International classification of financial reporting
reporting

Routledge series on international accounting and finance
Edited by C. W. Nobes
Coopers Deloitte Professor of Accounting, University of Reading

International Classification of Financial Reporting: Second Edition
Christopher Nobes

International Accounting: A Survey
J. M. Samuels and A. G. Piper

Accountants' Liability in the 1980s: An International View
E. P. Minnis and C. W. Nobes

Financial Reporting in India
Claire Marston

Multinational Accounting: Segment, Disclosure and Risk
Bimal Prodhan

International Group Accounting: International Harmonisation and the Seventh EEC Directive
Edited by S. J. Gray and A. G. Coenenburg

Governmental Accounting and Auditing: International Comparisons
Edited by James L. Chan and Rowan H. Jones

Accounting in Socialist Countries
Edited by D. T. Bailey

International classification of financial reporting
Second edition

Christopher Nobes

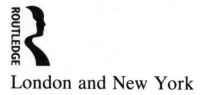

London and New York

First edition published 1984 by Croom Helm Ltd.
Second edition published 1992
by Routledge
11 New Fetter Lane, London EC4P 4EE

Simultaneously published in the USA and Canada
by Routledge
a division of Routledge, Chapman and Hall, Inc.
29 West 35th Street, New York, NY 10001

Typeset by J&L Composition Ltd, Filey, North Yorkshire
Printed and bound in Great Britain by
Mackays of Chatham PLC, Chatham, Kent

British Library Cataloguing in Publication Data
Nobes, Christopher
    International classification of financial reporting.
    – 2nd ed. – (International accounting and finance)
    I. Title II. Series
    657.3

Library of Congress Cataloging in Publication Data
Nobes, Christopher.
    International classification of financial reporting /
Christopher Nobes. – 2nd ed.
        p. cm. – (Routledge series on international accounting
and finance)
    Includes bibliographical references and index.
    ISBN 0–415–07090–2
    1. Comparative accounting – Classification.   2. Financial
statements.   I. Title.   II. Series.
    HF5625.N63   1992
    657′.3′012–dc20   91–25880
                                                                              CIP

ISBN 0–415–07090–2

Contents

Figures

Tables

Preface to the first edition

In late 1975, a few months after I had arrived at the University of Exeter to take up my first academic post, I decided to try to make comparative international accounting my special area of interest. My colleague, Pat Kirkman, suggested that I write for advice to Professor R. H. Parker of the University of Dundee. That I had never heard that name before is a clear demonstration of how unsullied my practising accountant's mind was with things academic. A few months later, it became clear that this man was to be the first professor of accountancy at the University of Exeter. The muses had looked down upon me with an unusually broad smile, and dealt me a stroke of such good luck that I will likely never recover from it.

I here acknowledge that this work owes much to the guidance and encouragement of Bob Parker, both in the germination of ideas over several years and during the writing. I have also benefitted greatly from the statistical and computer processing skills of John Matatko, Sue King and Bernard Pearson. John Matatko suggested the programs used, and helped to explain the results reported, on p. 69. Bernard Pearson provided the programs shown on pp. 71 and 80. Sue King turned my data into a suitable meal for the machine, and made sure that it obeyed our instructions.

I am also very grateful to Paul Rutteman of Arthur Young and Co. for putting me in contact with members of his firm's offices in six European countries. I received great assistance in those offices in April and May 1981. I also acknowledge the many useful comments of Dr Ian Stewart of the University of Auckland and Professor Sid Gray of the University of Glasgow on earlier drafts.

The persons who carried out one of the most onerous tasks were

Mrs Elvy Ibbotson and Miss Susanne Robertson who typed many drafts of this work. For this I record hearty thanks.

This book is a substantial extract from my PhD thesis of 1982.

Christopher Nobes
University of Strathclyde
July 1983

Preface to the second edition

Much has changed since the first edition of this book in July 1983. In the European Community (EC) the Fourth and Seventh Directives have been implemented in most countries. Spain and Portugal have joined the EC. The IASC has issued several more standards and has become a more powerful body. The standard-setting authorities in the UK and in Australia have changed. Globalization of the securities markets has continued. The Big-9 have become the Big-6, although they are still commonly referred to as the Big-8. Several papers have been published in the area of harmonization and classification. Further useful comments have been made on my classification scheme. All of this has led to the need to amend the first edition, although some material has been left unaltered where appropriate.

Whereas the first edition was prepared and processed in Exeter and Strathclyde Universities, this one was worked on in Sydney and Reading Universities.

Christopher Nobes

1 Introduction

This book examines the causes and nature of the differences between financial reporting practices in different countries; it asks whether classification of those countries by such practices is possible and useful; it critically appraises the attempts of other researchers; and proposes an hypothetical classification which is to be tested in several different ways.

Chapter 2 examines those factors which may reasonably be supposed to be the causes of differences in financial reporting practices. In some cases, these suggested causes stretch back over centuries, for example, the nature of the legal system or the degree of centralization of a country. Other long-run factors are the type of ownership of business and thus the predominant users of accounting information. These and other factors are used in an attempt to explain the diversity of accounting practices. Chapter 2 approaches these differences by subject matter; for example, it looks at conservatism and consolidation across countries. Having seen that large variations in financial reporting exist, it seems natural to ask whether countries may be usefully classified into groups by these differences.

Chapter 3 examines what have been seen to be the purposes of classification in other disciplines. In many, classification has played an early and fundamental role in organized, scientific research. Examples of classification in chemistry, biology, languages, law, economics and politics are examined. The problems met and the rules found useful in these other disciplines are studied to see if they might apply to comparative accounting.

Chapter 4 critically appraises the 'subjective' classifications of several other researchers. Some of these are merely untested speculations; most are somewhat vague and merely divide some parts of the world into a few groups with specification of a few examples of each group; some are based so heavily on business background factors that they must not be expected to apply to accounting practices. Professor Mueller's (1967) four-group classification perhaps stands out as a useful basis on which to build further.

Deeming these attempts to be unsatisfactory, other researchers have used the large database of Price Waterhouse surveys to carry out 'empirical' classifications. Chapter 5 critically examines the data, methodology and results of three such groups of researchers. This examination leads to the conclusion that there are serious problems with the data, which contains errors and was not designed for this purpose; with the methodology, which generates a classification rather than testing it; and thus with the resulting groups which vary by researcher, are implausible in some cases and lack detail in all cases. Nevertheless, the classifications by Nair and Frank (1980) seem to have been skilfully carried out and are plausible.

Chapter 6 tries to put into effect improvements suggested as a result of the criticisms made in chapter 5. First, a tighter definition of the classification is proposed. The author's hypothetical classification concerns the measurement and valuation practices relating to the financial reporting of listed companies in Western developed countries in 1980. An hypothetical classification with a hierarchy, which includes eighteen such countries, is presented. It is tested against the Price Waterhouse data. This is done using the methods of the research examined in chapter 5, and also using alternative 'clustering' programs. Considerable support for the classification may be found.

Chapter 7 relies on an entirely different set of data: one generated by the author. Nine factors which are deemed to represent important differential aspects of the fundamental nature of financial reporting are chosen. Then, a scoring of each of fourteen countries on each factor is carried out. This is open to inspection. These data are then used to produce clusters using several different computer programs.

Chapter 8 summarizes the first five chapters and draws conclusions from the following two chapters on a new proposed classification. There is also a discussion on the links between classification and harmonization.

Chapter 9 (which is new in this edition) analyses some of the relevant developments in these areas in the 1980s.

2 International differences in accounting

There seems to be a broad consensus about many of the factors which are related to international differences in accounting. That these factors *cause* the differences is an hypothesis made here. Unfortunately, it is an hypothesis which is difficult to test. Nevertheless, relationships between factors and accounting practices may be empirically established, and causality from the former to the latter seems plausible.

This chapter considers these factors and then examines some important structural differences. The analysis here is used as background material for the discussion of international classifications of the accounting practices of different countries in later chapters.

CAUSES OF DIFFERENCE

This present work is mainly devoted to financial reporting systems of commercial companies in developed Western countries, thus discussion of the causes of difference will be within this context. Some researchers have used impressions of such causes as input to the process of differentiating between countries (Mueller 1967). Other researchers have studied whether perceived differences in accounting practices correlate with such perceived causal factors (Frank 1979). In general, the factors discussed and confirmed are a standard set and, not surprisingly, correspond with common sense. Such factors which are seen as influencing accounting development include the nature of the legal system, the prevalent types of business organization and ownership, the influence of taxation and the strength of the accounting profession.

Other factors, like language or geography, have been referred to by the above-mentioned researchers. To the extent that these do have some explanatory power, it seems more sensible to assume that this results from auto-correlation. That is, the fact that Australian accounting bears a marked resemblance to New Zealand accounting might be 'confirmed' by language and geographical factors. However, most of their accounting similarities were not *caused* by these factors, but by their historical connection with the UK which passed on both accounting and language, and was colonizing most parts of Australasia in the same period.

Six factors which may be seen as important causes of international differences between financial reporting systems are examined below.

Legal systems

Some countries have a legal system which relies upon a limited amount of statute law, which is then interpreted by courts which build up large amounts of case law to supplement the statutes. Such a 'common law' system was formed in England primarily by post-conquest judges acting on the king's behalf. It is less abstract than codified law (see below); a common law rule seeks to provide an answer to a specific case rather than to formulate a general rule for the future. Although this common law system emanates from England, it may be found in similar forms in many countries influenced by England. Thus, the federal law of the USA, the laws of Canada, Australia and so on are to a greater or lesser extent modelled on English common law. This naturally influences company law, which does not prescribe a large number of detailed, all-embracing rules to cover the behaviour of companies and how they should publish their financial statements. To a large extent (at least up until the 1981 Companies Act in the UK), accounting within such a context is not dependent upon law.

Other countries have Romano-Germanic law which was based on the Roman *ius çivile* as compiled by Justinian in the sixth century and developed by European universities from the twelfth century. Here rules are linked to ideas of justice and morality, they become doctrine. The words '*dirigisme*' and 'codified law' may be associated with such a system. This difference has the important effect that company law or commercial codes need to make rules in detail for accounting and financial reporting. For example, to a large extent in Germany, company accounting is a branch of company law. Table 2.1 illustrates the way in which the developed Western world's legal systems divide between these two types. In some countries, *dirigisme* is compounded with centralization and a desire to control the economy. In this case, the existence of an 'accounting plan' is the result (see p. 23).

Table 2.1 Examples of countries in the two Western legal systems

Common Law	Romano-Germanic
England and Wales	France
Ireland	Italy
United States (federal and most states)	Germany
Canada	Spain
Australia	Netherlands
New Zealand	Brazil
India (to some extent)	Argentina

Note: The laws of Scotland, Israel, South Africa, Quebec and the Philippines embody elements of both systems

Business organization and ownership

The prevalent types of business organization and ownership also differ. In France, capital provided by the state and by banks is very significant, as are small businesses. In Germany, the banks in particular are important owners of companies. A majority of shares in some public companies are owned or controlled as proxies by banks, particularly by the Deutsche, Dresdner and Commerz Banks (Beeny 1975: 9–10; Lafferty 1975: 42–4). In many cases, in such countries the banks or the state will nominate directors and thus be able to obtain information and affect decisions.

Table 2.2 Listed companies, 1989

Stock exchange	Number of domestic listed companies
UK	1804
New York	1604
NASDAQ	4179
Germany (all exchanges)	609
Paris	459
Amsterdam	232
Milan	228

Source: Quality of Markets, ISE London, Autumn 1989

Another way of looking at this is that there are few listed companies with a widespread ownership of shares. Table 2.2 illustrates this by showing the number of listed shares in France and Germany and including for comparison the number for the UK and the USA. The divide is as obvious as that for legal systems, and can be expanded to include most of the countries in table 2.1 in the same two groups (taking account of size of economy or population). This factor is further discussed under 'Stock exchanges' (see p. 7).

Table 2.3 Institutional shareholdings

| | % of equities held by institutions | |
	UK	USA
1963	26	23
1969	37	–
1975	52	34
1978	49	–
1980	60	41

Source: Sibley (1981): 118, 119

Although it is increasingly the case that shares in countries like the UK and the USA are held by institutional investors rather than by individual shareholders (see table 2.3), this still contrasts with state, bank or family holdings. Indeed, the increased importance of institutional investors is perhaps a reinforcement for the following hypothesis: in countries with a widespread ownership of companies by shareholders who do not have access to internal information there will be pressure for disclosure, audit and 'fair' information. Institutional investors hold larger blocks of shares and may be better organized than private shareholders, thus their desire for information and their command of resources should increase this pressure, although they may also be able successfully to press for insider information.

'Fair' is difficult to define (Flint 1982). It is a concept related to those large number of outside owners who require unbiased information about the success of the business and its state of affairs (Stamp 1980). Although reasonable prudence will be expected, these shareholders are interested in comparing one year with another and one company with another, thus the accruals concept and some degree of realism will be required. This entails judgement which entails experts. This expertise is also required for the checking of the financial statements by auditors. Over many decades this can result in a tendency to require accountants to work out their own technical rules. The latter is acceptable to governments because of the influence and expertise of the accounting profession, which is usually running ahead of the interest of the government (as shareholder, protector of public interest or collector of taxation). Thus, 'generally accepted accounting principles' control accounting. To the extent that governments intervene, they impose disclosure, filing or measurement requirements which tend to follow best practice rather than to create it.

Returning to those continental European countries where there are fewer individually held shares, if there had been no government interference there might have been little or no accounting for persons other than managers. Governments have been prompted to call for information in order to try to control the economy or the tax system.

Stock exchanges

Just as the importance of government as a user of accounting information leads to a strong influence of taxation or accounting plan rules, so the importance of shareholders is connected with stock exchange activities. Where private shareholders have traditionally been important, some stock exchange regulations on disclosure are to be found, but these are comparatively minor. The profession and even the law has usually moved ahead, influenced by shareholders' needs. Such is the case in the UK, Australia, Canada and, to some extent, the Netherlands. The clear exception is the USA, where a breakdown of the financial system in 1929/30 led to government interference in the form of the Securities and Exchange Commission (SEC) formed in 1933 and subject to Congress. However, even here, the setting of detailed accounting rules has generally been left to accountants. A National Companies and Securities Commission has been set up in Australia, and has led to a partial loss of control over standards by the profession.

In continental European countries there were until recently no effective bodies acting on behalf of the relatively unimportant private shareholders. However, in France and Italy the governments have stepped in to create bodies to oversee the exchanges. In each case, this has led to important developments in financial reporting for listed companies, nearly always in the direction of existing Anglo-Saxon practice. This is not surprising as these stock exchange bodies are taking the part of private and institutional shareholders who have, over a much longer period, helped to shape Anglo-Saxon accounting systems.

In France the *Commission des Opérations de Bourse* (COB) was formed in 1968. Its officers are appointed by the government. It is charged with encouraging the growth of the Bourse by improving the quality of published information and the operations of the market. It has established listing requirements and has investigated cases of non-compliance with publication and disclosure requirements. Perhaps its most obvious campaign has been that to introduce consolidation. In 1968, consolidation was extremely rare, even for listed companies. As table 2.4 shows, matters improved substantially under pressure from COB, including a requirement to consolidate for all companies wishing to obtain a new listing.

Table 2.4 Number of listed French companies publishing financial statements

	At least a consolidated balance sheet	Consolidated balance sheet plus consolidated profit and loss account
1967	22	15
1968	44	25
1969	64	39
1970	74	42
1971	104	76
1972	163	121
1973	216	161
1974	232	183
1975	267	213
1976	292	246
1977	319	267
1978	328	289
1979	351	305
1980	364	332
1981	363	344

Source: Commission des Opérations de Bourse, Annual Reports

Although there are far fewer listed companies in Italy than there are in France (see table 2.2) the effect of the *Commissione Nazionale per le Società a la Borsa* (CONSOB) may be even greater than that of COB, partly because of the much less satisfactory state of affairs in Italy before CONSOB's formation in June 1974. CONSOB has powers to call for consolidation or extra disclosures which it has not used extensively yet. However, its real influence is linked to the Presidential Decree No. 126 of March 1975 which, after much delay, was introduced by statutory instrument. This requires listed companies to have a more extensive audit, undertaken by an auditing company approved by CONSOB. This requirement is in addition to the statutory audit by *sindaci* or state registered auditors. Its introduction was phased, with the largest listed companies complying by 1982, followed by smaller listed companies and banks.

In order to strengthen the hand of the new auditors, the Italian professional body, the *Ordine dei Dottore Commercialisti* has set up a committee to issue accounting and auditing principles (*principi contabili* and *principi di revisione*). These principles have been issued since 1979. They are advisory for listed companies and others. The committee contains representatives from Anglo-American firms, and the accounting principles bear considerable resemblance to Anglo-Saxon practice and thus to the standards of the International Accounting Standards Committee. Further, partly because the commercial code is widely drawn, there are no substantial inconsistencies between the code and the new principles. There are, of course, differences between the principles and the fiscal laws. This problem is yet to be resolved. However, it is clear that the government, CONSOB and the *Ordine* are in favour of it when implementing the 'true and fair' provisions of the EC's Fourth Directive on company law.

The government itself in 1981 issued obligatory accounting principles for use by the many state controlled companies, some of which are very large. Again, advice was sought from Anglo-American firms and the resulting principles, though different in some respects from the *principi contabili* of the *Ordine*, represent a significant shift towards 'fair' accounting.

All this change creates a problem for the process of classification of Italian accounting with the systems of other countries. There are more details on Italian accounting in appendix II.

Taxation

Although it is possible to make groupings of tax systems in a number of ways, only some of them are of relevance to accounting. For example, it is easy to divide most of the developed Western countries into those using 'classical' and those using 'imputation' systems of corporation tax (James and Nobes 1988). However, this distinction does not affect accounting. What is much more relevant is the degree to which taxation regulations determine accounting measurements (see appendix III). To some extent this can be revealed in a negative way by studying the problem of deferred taxation, which is caused by timing differences between tax and accounting treatments. In the UK and the USA, for example, the problem of deferred tax has caused much controversy and a considerable amount of accounting standard documentation. Turning to Germany and Sweden, it is found that the problem does not really exist to be solved; for in these latter countries it is to a large extent the case that the tax rules *are* the accounting rules. In Germany, the commercial accounts (*handelsbilanz*) should be the same as the tax accounts (*steuerbilanz*). There is even a word for this idea: the *massgeblichkeitsprinzip*.

One obvious example of the effects of this concerns depreciation. In the UK, the amount of depreciation charged in the published financial statements is determined according to custom established over the last century and influenced by the accounting standard, SSAP 12. The standard points out that:

Depreciation should be allocated to accounting periods so as to charge a fair proportion to each accounting period during the expected useful life of the asset . . . (para. 1). . . . The management of a business has a duty to allocate depreciation as fairly as possible to the periods expected to benefit from the use of the asset, and should select the method regarded as most appropriate to the type of asset and its use in the business.

The injunctions contained in the standard are of a fairly general nature, and their spirit is quite frequently ignored. For example, although it may not be clear which method is most suitable for a particular asset, it is unlikely that for 88 per cent of assets it was the straight line method (ICAEW 1980). Presumably, the prevalence of the straight line method is more related to the fact that it is simple and well established. Convention and pragmatism, rather than exact rules or even the spirit of the standard, also determine the method of judging the scrap value and the expected length of life.

The amount of depreciation for *tax* purposes in the UK is quite independent of these figures. It is determined by capital allowances, which are a formalized scheme of tax depreciation allowances designed to standardize the amounts allowed and to act as investment incentives. Because of the separation of the two schemes, there can be a complete lack of subjectivity in tax allowances but full room for judgement in financial depreciation charges.

At the opposite extreme, in countries like Germany, the tax regulations lay down depreciation rates to be used for particular assets. These are generally based on the expected useful lives of assets (see appendix III). However, in some cases, accelerated depreciation allowances have been available: for example, for industries producing energy-saving or anti-pollution products or for those operating in West Berlin or other areas that bordered East Germany. If these allowances are to be claimed for tax purposes (which would normally be sensible), they must be charged in the financial accounts. Thus, the charge against profit would be said by a UK accountant not to be 'fair', even though it could certainly be 'correct' or 'legal'. This influence is felt even in the details of the choice of method of depreciation, as an extract from a German annual report shows: 'Plant and machinery are depreciated over a useful life of ten years on a declining-balance basis; straight-line depreciation is adopted as soon as this results in a higher charge'. (AEG Telefunken 1986: 23 quoted here.)

A second example of the overriding effect of taxation on accounting measurement is the valuation of fixed assets in France. In principle, French companies have always been allowed to revalue assets. However, this would normally have entailed extra taxation due to the increase in the post-revaluation balance sheet total compared to the previous year's. In continental countries, such value adjustments may not be put directly to reserves. Consequently, except in the special case of merger by *fusion* when tax-exempt revaluation is allowed, revaluation was not practised. However, the Finance Acts of 1978 and 1979 made revaluation obligatory for listed companies and for those which solicit funds from the public; it was optional for others (van Waardenburg 1979). The purpose was to show balance sheets more realistically. The revaluation was performed by the use of government indices relating to 31 December 1976. The credit goes to an undistributable revaluation reserve. For depreciable assets, an amount equal to the extra depreciation due to revaluation is *credited* to profit and loss and *debited* to the revaluation account. Thus the effect of revaluation on profit (*and tax*) is neutralized. This move from no revaluations to compulsory revaluations is due to the change in tax rules.

Further examples are easy to find: bad debt provisions (determined by tax laws in many continental countries), development and maintenance expenditures (carried forward for tax purposes in Spain) or various provisions related to specific industries (see extract from CFP annual report under 'Provisions and reserves' on p. 19).

The effects of all this are to reduce the room for operation of the accruals convention (which is the driving force behind such practices as depreciation) and to reduce 'fairness'. Until the legislation following the EC's Fourth Directive, the importance of this effect was not disclosed in published accounts. With some variations, this *massgeblichkeitsprinzip* operates in Germany, France, Belgium, Italy, Spain, Japan and many other countries. It is perhaps due partly to the persuasive influence of codification in law, and partly to the predominance of taxation as a cause of accounting.

The alternative approach, exemplified above by the UK, is found in countries with an older tradition of published accounting, where commercial rules have come first. Most of the countries on the left in table 2.1 are, to varying degrees, like this. In most cases, there is not the degree of separation between tax and financial accounting that is found in the UK in the shape of capital allowances.

However, in all such countries the taxation authorities have to adjust the commercial accounts for their own purposes, after exerting only minor influences directly on them. One example of such influences was the encouragement to the use of LIFO (last in first out) for stock valuation in the USA by its being allowed by the Internal Revenue Service; the important point being that it had to be used in financial accounts if used for tax purposes. In the UK, there is only an indirect effect in this area; since LIFO is not accepted by the Revenue this reinforces (and antedates) its prohibition by accounting standard (SSAP 9).

An interesting exception to the pattern of countries that appear to be clearly emerging from the factors discussed so far in this chapter is the Netherlands. Although the Netherlands has a Romano-Germanic legal system and few listed companies, if one studies its commercial maritime history it bears considerable similarities to England's. Also, although the number of listed companies is small, some of those companies are very large (e.g. Philips, Akzo, Royal Dutch, Unilever, Hoogovens) and are the basis of an active stock exchange. At any rate, when it comes to taxation and many other factors related to accounting, the Netherlands appears to fit well with what one might call the Anglo-Saxon as opposed to the continental European group.

Further, Denmark deliberately moved from a Germanic to an Anglo-American system after World War II.

The profession

The strength, size and competence of the accountancy profession in a country may follow to a large extent from the various factors outlined above and from the type of accounting they have helped to produce. For example, the lack of a substantial body of private shareholders and public companies in some countries means that the need for auditors is much smaller than it is in the UK and the USA. However, the nature of the profession also feeds back into the type of accounting that is practised and *could* be practised. For example, as has been mentioned, the 1975 decree in Italy (not brought into effect until the 1980s) requiring listed companies to have extended audits similar to those operated in Anglo-Saxon countries could only be implemented initially because of the substantial presence of Anglo-Saxon accounting firms. This factor constitutes a considerable obstacle to any attempts at significant and deep harmonization of accounting between some countries.

The scale of the difference is illustrated in table 2.5. These remarkable figures need some interpretation. For example, there follows a more careful comparison of the German and British figures. First, in Germany there is a separate, though overlapping, profession of tax experts (*Steuerberater* and *Steuerbevollmätigte*), which is larger than the accounting body. Even in the USA, many tax experts are lawyers. However, in the UK the 'accountants' figure is especially inflated by the inclusion of many who specialize in or occasionally practise in tax. Second, a German accountant may only be a member of the *Institut* if he or she is in practice, whereas at least half of the British figure represents members in commerce, industry, government, education and so on. Third, the training period is much longer in Germany than it is in the UK. It normally involves a four-year relevant degree course, six years practical experience (four in the profession) and a professional examination consisting of oral and written tests plus a thesis. This tends to last until the aspiring accountant is 30 to 35 years old. Thus, many of the German 'students' would be counted as part of the qualified figure if they were in the British system.

A more recent factor is the creation in the mid-1980s of a second tier body of auditors, allowed to audit the accounts of private companies: the *vereidigte Buchprüfer*.

Table 2.5 Public accountancy bodies, age and size, 1988

Country	Body	Founding date*	Approx. nos. in thousands
United States	American Institute of Certified Public Accountants	1887	264
Canada	Institute of Chartered Accountants of Canada	1902 (1880)	44
United Kingdom and Ireland	Institute of Chartered Accountants in England and Wales	1880 (1870)	87
	Institute of Chartered Accountants of Scotland	1951 (1854)	12
	Association of Certified Accountants	1939 (1891)	30
	Institute of Chartered Accountants in Ireland	1888	6
Australia	Australian Society of Accountants	1952 (1887)	57
	Institute of Chartered Accountants in Australia	1928 (1886)	18
France	Ordre des Experts Comptables et des Comptables Agréés	1942	11
Germany	Institut der Wirtschaftsprüfer	1932	5
Netherlands	Netherlands Instituut van Register-accountants	1895	6

* *Dates of earliest predecessor bodies in brackets*

These four factors help to explain the differences. However, there is still a very substantial residual difference which results from the much larger number of companies to be audited and the more lengthy process of forming a judgement on the 'fair' view.

It is interesting to note a further division along Anglo-Saxon *v.* continental European lines. In the former, governments require certain types of companies to be audited, and put certain limits on who shall be auditors, with government departments having the final say. However, in general, membership of the recognized professional accountancy bodies is the starting point. However, in France and Germany there is a dual set of accountancy bodies. Those in table 2.5 are not the bodies to which one must belong to qualify as an auditor of companies, though to a large extent the memberships of these professional bodies overlap with the auditing bodies, and membership of the former enables membership of the latter. The bodies are shown in table 2.6. The professional bodies set exams, consider ethical matters, belong to the international accounting bodies, and so on. The auditing bodies are run by the state. The *Compagnie Nationale* is responsible to the Ministry of Justice; the *Wirtschaftsprüferkammer* to the Federal Minister of Economics.

This system is the basis for the EC's Eighth Directive which is being implemented throughout the Community.

Table 2.6 Accountancy bodies in France and Germany

	Professional body	*State auditing body*
France:	Ordre des Experts Comptables	Compagnie Nationale des Commissaires aux Comptes
Germany:	Institut der Wirtschaftsprüfer	Wirtschaftsprüferkammer

Other influences

Many other influences have been at work in shaping accounting practices. Some are not indirect and subtle like the type of ownership of companies, but direct and external to accounting like the enactment of new laws. For example, the economic crisis in the USA in the late 1920s and early 1930s produced a number of Securities Acts which have diverted accounting from its previous course by introducing extensive disclosure requirements and control (usually by threat only) of accounting standards. As other examples, the proposed introduction into Italy of Anglo-Saxon accounting principles by choice of the government, and into Luxembourg of consolidation and detailed disclosure as a result of EC directives are against all previous trends there. In Spain, the 'artificial' adoption of the accounting plan from France follows that latter country's adoption of it after pressure by the occupying Germans in the early 1940s. Perhaps most obvious and least natural is the adoption of various British Companies Acts or International Accounting Standards by developing countries with a negligible number of the sort of public companies or private shareholders which have given rise to the accounting practices contained in these laws or standards.

There has also been a strong influence in a few cases from theory, perhaps most obviously in the case of micro-economics in the Netherlands. Accounting theorists there had proposed that the users of financial statements would be given the fairest view of the performance and state of affairs of an individual company by allowing accountants to use judgement in the context of that particular company to select and present accounting figures. In particular, it was suggested that replacement cost information might give the best picture. The looseness of law and tax requirements, and the receptiveness of the profession to micro-economic ideas (no doubt partly because of their training by the academic theorists) has led to the present diversity of practice, the emphasis on 'fairness' through judgement, and the experimentation with and practice of replacement cost accounting.

Conclusion

This section has discussed some of the influences on the development of accounting practices. The importance of the mix of users of accounting information seems clear; it has a large part to play in the emergence of the dominant source of rules for accounting practice. In many continental European countries, the importance of governments as collectors of taxation or controllers of the economy, has led to the dominance of company laws, commercial codes and tax regulations. In Anglo-Saxon countries, the effective control of accounting practice has been exercised by the accounting profession. This was first seen as a vague corpus of 'best' or 'accepted' practices, and later has been refined with the issue of detailed accounting standards. However, these standards are still loosely drawn documents which permit considerable flexibility and the use of judgement. The interests of private shareholders as users of financial statements has been a continuing background pressure on the profession as it develops standard practice.

NATURE OF DIFFERENCES

To some extent the nature of the differences in financial accounting has already been described above. Certainly the taxation effects are not just influences towards differences but amount to differences *per se*. Other differences are examined below.

Conservatism

Perhaps because of the different mix of users in different countries, conservatism is of differing strength in the countries considered here. For example, the importance of banks in Germany may explain the greater conservatism in reporting. It is widely held that bankers are more interested in 'rock bottom' figures in order to satisfy themselves that long-term loans are safe. At the same time, the consequent lack of those interested in a 'fair' view reduces the importance of the accruals convention which would normally modify conservatism.

In the UK it is more usual to refer to the concept of 'prudence' (as in SSAP 2). In many cases, accounting standards are the compromise treaties which settle a battle between conservatism and the accruals concept. For example, it is not fully conservative to allow the capitalization of some development expenditure as in SSAP 13, but it may still be prudent. A similar argument applies to the taking of profit on long-term contracts as in SSAP 9, or to the partial accounting for deferred tax (SSAP 15). Many other Anglo-Saxon countries and the Netherlands use a similar concept, although US accounting practice does not go quite this far. It does not allow capitalization of development expenditure (FAS 2), and insists on full tax allocation (APB 11).

Nevertheless, continental European conservatism is clearly of a more stringent variety. For example, the following features are to be found in German accounting even after the implementation of the EC's Fourth Directive in 1985:

(a) Legal (undistributable) reserves of 10 per cent of share capital are required to be built up out of profits (5 per cent per year allocations of profit).
(b) Profit on long-term contracts must wait until completion, unlike the Anglo-Saxon 'percentage of completion basis', as in the UK's SSAP 9.
(c) Foreign currency debtors or creditors are not valued at year end rates but at the worse of year end and transaction rates.

(d) Stocks are valued at the lowest of historical cost, current replacement cost, net realizable value, or other lower value allowed by
tax rules.

(e) Hidden or secret reserves are approved of, particularly for
banks.

(f) Strict historical cost is used, as discussed below.

Some of these features are shared by most other continental
countries.

As a postscript, it may be noted that investment analysts are said to
increase greatly a German company's profit figure by a series of
adjustments before comparing it to a UK figure (Beeny 1975: ch. 4).
However, matters have 'improved' somewhat since the 1965 *Aktiengesetz*. Before that, it was suggested that: 'If the non-existence of a
contingency cannot be absolutely determined, then in the interest of
protecting the creditor, it must be assumed that such a contingency
exists' (Semler 1962).

This greater conservatism in continental Europe seems to be a
long-run feature. Davidson and Kohlmeier (1966) and Abel (1969)
noted that profit figures would be consistently lower in France,
Sweden, Germany and the Netherlands (when use of replacement
cost was assumed) if similar companies' accounts were merely
adjusted for differences in inventory and depreciation practices from
those used in the USA or the UK.

Gray (1980) suggests a measure of greater conservatism for
Germany and France. Touche Ross (1989) also provide examples of
this.

Historical cost

Historical cost is a concept adhered to in varying degrees in accounting throughout the developed Western world. The only country
where it has been under serious threat is the Netherlands, where
some companies have *published* replacement cost information since
the early 1950s, where some companies have for some years presented
their main accounts in replacement cost terms, and where a draft bill
in 1980 was to make replacement cost information compulsory in
cases where replacement cost differed substantially from historical
cost. This is an extreme example of attempts to free accounting from
what many view as the serious distortion from 'fairness', for the
purposes of decision making, which is caused by historical cost
accounting. Nevertheless, even in the Netherlands, historical cost
remains predominant.

In many South American countries, partly because sufficiently elaborate indices are not available and because replacement cost accounting is subjective, high inflation has brought about the use of general purchasing power (GPP) adjusted accounting rather than replacement cost accounting (Kirkman 1991). Such GPP accounting is, of course, merely historical cost accounting with year-end adjustments using a government-published single index series.

Perhaps at the other extreme from the Netherlands is the rigid approach of consistent, exact and unsupplemented historical cost accounting as used in Germany. Although the USA uses a strict approach to historical cost accounting, this has been added to by experiments in the late 1970s by the Securities and Exchange Commission (SEC) and the Financial Accounting and Standards Board (FASB) in the shape of requirements for listed and large companies to produce replacement cost and general purchasing power information.

Between the extremes of the German and Dutch practice have been the rather relaxed attitude in the UK towards revaluation within 'historical cost' accounts coupled with halting steps towards replacement cost, and the French, Greek and Spanish organized revaluations. Thus the picture here is very confused, particularly for listed companies, who have borne the brunt of experimentation in various countries. Even by concentrating on what *does* happen rather than what is theoretically *allowed* to happen, and on listed companies, and on main accounts, it still seems to be impossible to draw a diagram of the relative positions of countries. Does the fiscal revaluation of the late 1970s in France mean that French accounting is more affected by replacement cost than British accounting? Perhaps the only factor that does emerge clearly is rather unfortunate for the consistency of the case implied in the preceding pages of this chapter about the similarities between the influences on UK and US accounting. It appears to be difficult to group the UK with the USA on adherence to historical cost. However, the progress of the two countries in the 1970s towards supplementary price-adjusted accounting looks remarkably similar. Perhaps this similarity in response to an external stimulus in the shape of inflation shows us how similar the underlying *system* is, and is more important than the fact that US accounting holds to a stricter interpretation of historical cost when it comes to the revaluation of fixed assets in the statutory accounts.

Provisions and reserves

The distinction between provisions and reserves is important for accounting measurement because the former are charges against profit, whereas the latter are appropriations of profit. The influences which lead to a proliferation of significant provisions appear to be conservatism and rigid but generous tax regulations. Both these factors have been discussed, and their effects on provisions mentioned. The result of such provision accounting may be that the accruals convention and 'fairness' are partially overridden; this in turn may result in income smoothing.

The use of accelerated depreciation in the financial accounts is an example of over-provision. The lack of provision for bad debts in a system where it is not allowed for tax purposes is an example of under-provision. Provisions for risks and contingencies which fluctuate in reverse relationship with profits are examples of income smoothing. This may be illustrated using the French and German annual reports referred to above.

The extracts used here relate to the 1970s, on which the original classification study was based. Similar extracts could be found for other companies or other European countries in later years. In the CFP 1978 annual report, there are the following remarks:

> Provisions for Depletion Allowance. This provision is drawn up from taxable income and is justified by the more or less rapid depletion of deposits and the necessity of reconstituting reserves ... (CFP) was not concerned with such regulations until it became subject to consolidated profit income tax in 1966. ... Under its second authorization, the company created a further provision of MF 700.
>
> (A6)

> Chartered Accountants' opinion ... 6. The profit of the parent company is stated after dealing with movements on the provisions for contingencies and exchange fluctuations. In the UK, these two provisions would be classified as reserves.
>
> (A20)

Perhaps even more revealing are the following quotations from annual reports specially prepared by CFP for Anglo-Saxon stock exchange dealings.

> Depreciation of property, plant and equipment was F2274 million vs F2283 million in 1976. Provision amounts were lower in 1977

than in 1976, especially because cash flow reflected on the French market did not allow constitution of a provision for foreign exchange fluctuations at the same level as in 1976.

(1977: 22)

Taking into account these items, income for the year was F111 million, to which must be added a deduction of F90 million from the Provision for contingencies. Income finally amounts to F201 million (1976 – F237 million) but includes lower exceptional income

(1977: 23)

Following the usual effect of amounts set aside to or written back from depreciation and provisions and an allocation of F800 million to reconstitute the provision for contingencies, net income for the year totalled F971 million (1978 – F266 million).

(1979: 23)

A useful comparison may also be made between the treatment of provisions in the statutory (parent company) accounts and their treatment of consolidated accounts which have been influenced by Anglo-Saxon practices (and auditors). This is clearer in earlier years, before fiscal revaluation. For the 1976 accounts, the comparison is shown in table 2.7. It reveals the greater tendency to treat items as provisions.

Turning to Germany, remarks concerning provisions have already been made in the section on conservatism. Two further brief quotations will suffice to show a parallel with French practices quoted above; both come from the 1986 annual report of AEG Telefunken, mentioned previously:

Provisions for pensions . . . have remained unchanged as compared to the previous year. . . . To hold the cover at the previous year's level of 80% would have required an additional provision of DM 58 million.

The decline in sundry provisions is attributable to the utilization of provisions set aside in previous years for possible liabilities in connection with the nuclear reactor contracts.

(34)

It appears that in Italy and Spain, the commercial codes (which would certainly allow greater use of the accruals convention) have been overridden to a large extent by the need to satisfy the requirements of tax inspectors. Only recently, have tax reforms and stronger

Table 2.7 Provisions and reserves, CFP, 1976, F000s

Statutory accounts		Consolidated accounts	
Reserves		*Reserves*	
Issued capital	1,068,690	Issued capital	1,068,690
Share premium	357 236	Share premium and other	4,371,287
Legal reserve	106 869	Legal reserve	106 869
General reserve	3,465,546		
Surplus on shares	14,335		
Revaluation reserve	30,170		
	5,042,848		
Provisions			
Contingencies	304,000		
Exchange fluctuations	200,000		
	5,546,846		5,546,846
Other contingencies	47,400		
Employees' investment	5,000		
		Provisions	
		Deferred taxes and other contingencies	2,059,480
		Staff pensions	235,934

Source: CFP Annual Report (1976): 49 and 63. Figures used are 1976 'after allocation'

accounting principles allowed the use of 'fairer' provisions of various types.

In the UK, provisions for depreciation and bad debts are not affected by tax requirements. Provisions for risks and contingencies are rare and usually associated with cases where a liability is fairly certain in incidence, if not in amount. Broadly speaking, these practices prevail in the rest of the Anglo-Saxon world and in the Netherlands. However, there is an important exception in the treatment of deferred tax, which is fully provided for in the USA, Canada, Australia and the Netherlands, but (since the late 1970s) not in the UK.

Consolidation

The practice of consolidation became widespread first in the USA and then in the UK during the inter-war years (Kitchen 1972; Walker 1978). It grew up with the increase of holding companies, in order to avoid what was seen as misrepresentation of balance sheets which only contained investments at cost, and profit and loss accounts which only contained dividends from controlled companies. There is general agreement on the main procedures of consolidation in the

Anglo-Saxon world and the Netherlands; in which countries consolidation for subsidiaries is almost universal practice. However, the
practices are not consistent with any one theory of consolidation
(Walker 1978: ch. 15), and the details of the treatment of inter-
company profit and many other matters vary. Further, while there is
some consensus about the definition and treatment of *associated
companies*, there are variations; in Australia practice is not uniform.
Nevertheless, this set of countries seems to have been influenced
heavily by the needs of outside users of the accounts of groups of
companies towards the comprehensive use of consolidation. In
general, this practice preceded legal or professional requirements. It
is only when the practices of this set are compared to those of other
countries that the appearance of homogeneity in this first set becomes
very strong.

Back in 1980, when the original classification project was carried
out, consolidation was either a recent development or still rare in
much of continental Europe. In Germany, consolidation had been
made compulsory by the 1965 *Aktiengesetz* for public companies.
However, foreign subsidiaries were exempt and the equity method
for associates was illegal. Goodwill was calculated on the basis of
book values, and recalculated at each year end.

In France, until the late 1980s, there was no law on consolidation.
Thus, consolidation had been very rare because the profession and
user groups traditionally had no power. However, the formation of
COB in the late 1960s and the influence of Anglo-Saxon practices,
due to the presence of Anglo-American firms and the desire of some
French companies for listings on the exchanges of London or New
York, caused a gradual increase in consolidation by listed companies.
This was illustrated earlier in table 2.4. Naturally, in a country
where there is no tradition of professional accounting measurement
standards, practice was very varied in cases where there was no law or
tax requirements. The *Conseil National de la Comptabilité*, a government body with responsibility for the *plan*, issued guidelines in 1968
as follows: global consolidation should be used for holdings of over 50
per cent or where full control is exercised; *mise en équivalence*
(similar to equity method) for holdings of over 1/3 and at a lower
level if judged appropriate; proportional consolidation for companies
held by two or more groups and not by the public. However, these
guidelines were not followed exactly.

The CFP 1978 accounts (A9) stated that the equity method is used
in cases where the holding is 20 per cent or more. The information on
pages A15 and A16 seems to contradict this. In 1976 the equity

method was used down to 10 per cent holdings, and full consolidation in some cases where holdings were below 30 per cent (1976 annual reports: 44 and 45).

The EC Seventh Directive was implemented in Germany in 1985 and in France in 1986, coming into force in a variety of years for different companies etc., up until 1990. In Spain this occurs by the end of 1991; in Portugal, consolidation was non-existent even in 1990 and no date had been fixed for a change.

Uniformity and accounting plans

Such features as the lack of uniformity of accounting practice between companies in the Netherlands, as opposed to the emphasis on uniformity for government control of the economy in France have been mentioned earlier in this chapter. This area of difference needs to be discussed in more detail.

In France, the needs of the Economics Ministry in its role as controller of the French economy were seen to be well served by the use of accounting plans introduced by the occupying German forces in the early 1940s. Consequently, such a system has been in use in France throughout the post-war years. The first full version of the *plan comptable général* was produced in 1947, and revised versions were issued in 1957 and 1982. The *plan* exists in many versions for different industries. It comprises a chart of accounts, definitions of terms, model financial statements and rules for measurement and valuation. Thus, its influence is all-pervasive. The chart must be completed each year for national statistics purposes; the tax returns are based on the plan; published financial statements use the model formats; and all the former use the standard definitions and measurement rules. The *plan* even stretches to cost and management accounting.

Its use for central statistical purposes is very obvious. A government economist in Paris can collect charts for all companies and add together all amounts under a particular decimalized code in order to find the total investment in a particular type of fixed asset, defined in a standardized way. Naturally, as the government is historically the main user of accounting information in its capacities as economic controller, tax collector and provider of state capital, the *plan* is controlled by a government body: the *Conseil National de la Comptabilité*.

In Belgium, part of the process of preparing for the implementation of the Fourth Directive during the 1970s was the introduction of a compulsory accounting plan in 1976, not dissimilar from the French one. The Belgians had used a chart of accounts for some industries during the inter-war years, and had experienced full use of it during the early 1940s. In Spain, too, as appendix II discusses in more detail, an accounting plan based on the French has been introduced. In Germany, the use of charts of accounts is voluntary. In several developing countries influenced by France, the OCAM plan is used. Portuguese and Greek accounting also uses plans.

In those countries where the use of an accounting plan is compulsory, the degree of uniformity of presentation and measurement practices is much higher than in Anglo-Saxon countries. In Germany, without a compulsory accounting plan, the same effect is achieved in some areas by detailed laws and tax regulations. In Sweden, especially, uniformity and government control of accounting is used to enhance the ability to control the economy (Choi and Mueller 1978: 38–40, 113–14). In many developing countries, particularly those not directly influenced by the UK or the USA, accounting plans have been introduced. It may well be that, in the absences of large and listed companies, of many private shareholders and of a strong profession, the use of an accounting plan is more suitable than Anglo-Saxon judgemental accounting principles.

In countries using Anglo-Saxon type accounting, there is generally much less uniformity, but this does vary from one country to another. It has been mentioned that accounting in the Netherlands is without detailed rules. At the extremes, this manifests itself by the use of replacement cost accounting as statutory accounts by some companies, while others still use unsupplemented historical cost. In the 1970s the Dutch professional body, in concert with the employers' and employees' organizations began to issue 'observations' on accounting (*Beschouwingen*). These were not binding, but are part of the process of defining 'standards acceptable in economic and social life' as called for by the Act on the Annual Accounts of Enterprises, 1970. From 1981, somewhat more authoritative 'guidelines' (*Richtlijnen*) have been issued. Also in the Netherlands, there is a unique institution called the Enterprise Chamber (*Ondernemingskamer*) of the Court of Justice. This hears cases brought against companies or auditors under the 1970 Act. (For more details, see Klaassen 1980.)

Accounting in the UK, Ireland, Australia and New Zealand is rather more controlled than that in the Netherlands. Control is effected by sets of professionally issued accounting standards, which began to be published in the 1970s, and by company laws. The standards are binding on auditors and accountants but not on other directors. Thus, non-compliance is certainly possible but should lead to a qualified audit report. In 1990, the UK's Accounting Standards Board was set up independently from the professional bodies.

Further along the scale towards uniformity are the USA and Canada. In the USA, for companies within the scope of the SEC, the standards of the FASB are rather more powerful than UK accounting standards. The FASB is independent from (though influenced by) the accountancy profession, and has been delegated with the function of setting standards by the federal government-controlled SEC. The SEC refuses to accept for filing the financial statements of companies which have not obeyed 'generally accepted accounting principles', which normally means statements of the FASB and predecessor bodies. In Canada, the professional accountancy body's standards are similarly backed by the Business Corporations Act of 1975. This has generally meant the adoption by 'regulation' of the profession's standards.

This chapter has analysed the reasons for and the nature of the international differences in financial reporting. Before proceeding to examine classification of countries by these differences there is a general introduction to classification in chapter 3.

3 Introduction to classification

'What's the use of their having names', the Gnat said [referring to insects], 'if they won't answer to them?'

L. Carroll, *Through the Looking Glass*: ch. 3.

This chapter first discusses the purposes of classification in various disciplines, then looks at the rules which may be applied when classifying, then examines classifications in subjects other than accounting. It is hoped that such study will enable a better analysis of accounting classifications in the following chapters.

THE PURPOSE OF CLASSIFICATION

Classification was one of the earliest activities in the development of organized and scientific study in many disciplines. In the physical sciences it has been a basic tool of understanding. The Mendeleev table of elements (see figure 3.1) and the Linnaean system are fundamental to chemistry and biology. Such classifications 'sharpen description and analysis' (AAA 1977: 97) and help to reveal underlying structures. This enables prediction of the properties of a chemical element or an animal based on its place in a classification. For example, one could predict the behaviour of iodine from a study of chlorine and bromine and their relationship to iodine in figure 3.1. In some cases such a classification has predicted the existence of elements.

Further, in the physical sciences, classification has provided insights into what elements or animals once existed, might exist in the future or do exist and wait to be discovered. Chemists in the late nineteenth and early twentieth centuries searched for and found various elements predicted by the table of elements. Although taxonomy might be seen as an adolescent stage, physical scientists continually

1	2	3	4	5	6	7	8	9	10	11	12	13	14	15	16	17	18
1 H																	2 He
3 Li	4 Be											5 B	6 C	7 N	8 O	9 F	10 Ne
11 Na	12 Mg											13 Al	14 Si	15 P	16 S	17 Cl	18 Ar
19 K	20 Ca	21 Sc	22 Ti	23 V	24 Cr	25 Mn	26 Fe	27 Co	28 Ni	29 Cu	30 Zn	31 Ga	32 Ge	33 As	34 Se	35 Br	36 Kr
37 Rb	38 Sr	39 Y	40 Zr	41 Nb	42 Mo	43 Tc	44 Ru	45 Rh	46 Pd	47 Ag	48 Cd	49 In	50 Sn	51 Sb	52 Te	53 I	54 Xe
55 Cs	56 Ba	57 La	72 Hf	73 Ta	74 W	75 Re	76 Os	77 Ir	78 Pt	79 Au	80 Hg	81 Tl	82 Pb	83 Bi	84 Po	85 At	86 Rn
87 Fr	88 Ra	89 Ac	104 Rf	105 Ha													

58 Ce	59 Pr	60 Nd	61 Pm	62 Sm	63 Eu	64 Gd	65 Tb	66 Dy	67 Ho	68 Er	69 Tm	70 Yb	71 Lu
90 Th	91 Pa	92 U	93 Np	94 Pu	95 Am	96 Cm	97 Bk	98 Cf	99 Es	100 Pm	101 Md	102 No	103 Lr

Key For example

```
17
Cl
```

means { atomic number (e.g. numbers of protons) = 17
       { name of element = Chlorine

Figure 3.1 Periodic table of elements

rely upon it. Recently, physicists have been attempting to classify fundamental particles as an aid to understanding them, predicting their properties and searching for others.

The Mendeleev classification is uncontroversial, much neater and more stable than the biological classification. But taxonomy in biology retains its interest and central importance. It is this very lack of certainty which makes it of interest for scientists, too. From time to time, new animals are discovered or new theories propounded which cause revisions to the biological classification. As it can tell us much about classification problems in a complex area, the biological system will be examined in some detail later. Table 3.1 illustrates the detail to which the classification system can go by showing the full zoological hierarchy of the timber wolf of the Canadian subarctic.

Table 3.1 Zoological hierarchy of timber wolf

Kingdom: Animalia
Subkingdom: Metazoa
Phylum: Chordata
Subphylum: Vertebrata
Superclass: Tetrapoda
Class: Mammalia
Subclass: Theria
Infraclass: Eutheria
Cohort: Ferungulata
Superorder: Ferae
Order: Carnivora
Suborder: Fissipeda
Superfamily: Canoidea
Family: Canidae
Subfamily: Caninae
Tribe: none for this group
Genus: Canis
Subgenus: none for this group
Species: Canis Lupus
Subspecies: Canis Lupus Occidentalis

Note: Italicized taxa are obligatory, see p. 30 and table 3.2

Turning attention to international comparative study in the social sciences, it is found that researchers suffer from problems similar to those in any other area of social science work. That is, compared to the physical sciences, there is vagueness, uncertainty and a lack of progress in formulating generally agreed theories even on the most fundamental of matters. In accounting this is especially evident because of the recentness of the development of substantial research output.

However, there have been many international classification attempts in law, economics and politics. In the study of international comparative accounting, the classification stage has also been started but not successfully completed. Progress so far in this field will be outlined in the following chapters after a discussion of the rules that might be used for classification. Here, it may be said that the purposes of classification in the social sciences are analagous to some of those in the physical sciences. At the most basic level, there may be use, for example, in being able to define 'mixed economies' or 'centrally controlled economies' and then to refer to particular countries as falling into one classification or another.

In accounting, also, classification may be used as a way of describing and comparing different accounting systems. The activity involved in preparing a classification should encourage precision. A classifier should be led to examine the exact nature and importance of the differences and similarities between the accounting systems of different countries. The exercise should even improve understanding of a researcher's own national system, as it should involve the uncovering of the essential structure of a system from the mass of practical details.

A classification in accounting may also help to shape development rather than merely to describe how things are. For example, classification facilitates the study of the logic of and of the difficulties facing harmonization. Further, by studying a classification, a developing country might be better able to understand the available accounting systems, and which would be most appropriate for its own purposes.

For the teaching of students and for the training of accountants and auditors who move or deal internationally, a classification may prove very valuable. For example, US accountants wishing to learn about Belgian accounting might usefully start by noting that it is classified with French accounting rather than with Dutch accounting. Such a use may be particularly valuable for those with a peripheral interest in this field who find it hard enough to keep up with accounting in their own countries, without trying to understand accounting elsewhere.

For the profession or legislators in a country, it may be possible to use a classification to predict problems that may have to be faced, and to estimate the most suitable solutions by looking at other countries 'near' to it. It has even been suggested that a way of changing from one accounting system to another may be to adjust the economic and political parameters to those more conducive to the desired system (AAA 1977). However, this seems like trying to wag a tail by moving the dog.

Although a classification is a snap-shot, it will probably be misleading if it is regarded as a purely static exercise. It is clearly necessary to consider the history of accounting systems, the reasons for differences and their direction of movement at the moment of the snap-shot. (The next section discusses this further.) However, if the photographer includes the proper context, a series of stills can be taken over time to give a time-lapse study of the movements in a classification. This could prove to be a useful way of charting the progress of harmonization. It may be that a still taken in 1990 would show a clear shift from the 1980 picture. For example, accounting of the UK may move towards that of France and Germany and away from that of the USA. If so, this will be a sign of the progress of the EC harmonization programme.

RULES AND PROBLEMS WHEN CLASSIFYING

Types of classification

There are several ways of classifying. The simplest forms might be 'dichotomous grouping' (e.g. black things versus non-black things) or 'rank ordering' (e.g. by height of students in a class). More complex classifications include 'dimensioning' (e.g. the periodic table of elements) and 'systematizing' (e.g. the Linnaean system). Two ways of arriving at more complex classifications are 'multidimensional scaling' and 'morphological structuring'. The former uses two or more characteristics on different axes to try to find clusters of elements displaying similar characteristics. The latter seeks to compose a 'morphology' which lists elements by differentiating factors; it should then be clearer which elements are similar to each other (see figure 3.4 and tables 3.4 and 4.2).

Some rules in biological classification

Although table 3.2 shows a very large and apparently very ordered classification system, the number of ranks in the biological classification is not constant throughout, and the characteristics for classification do not stay the same throughout. However, there are rules, such as that a zoological species is a group of individuals that can breed among themselves but do not normally breed with other forms. Nevertheless, even such rules as this fail for micro-organisms which use non-sexual reproduction. Another rule of taxonomy is that certain ranks in the hierarchy are obligatory. This is illustrated for

Table 3.2 Obligatory hierarchy of ranks (example of man)

Kingdom: Animalia
Phylum: Chordata
Class: Mammalia
Order: Primates
Family: Hominidae
Genus: Homo
Species: Homo Sapiens

man in table 3.2. Great difficulties often occur when fitting a newly discovered animal into the classification, as mentioned below.

The need for judgement

Naturally, the above methods do not always lead to clear classifications. In chemistry, once ideas of atomic weights and numbers had been established, classification posed few problems. However, in biology the difficulties were and are considerable; and here there are close analogies with comparative accounting. Exactly which criteria should be used to classify and what weights to give them are matters of judgement. Members of a class resemble each other as cousins do, looking alike not because they all have one feature in common but because they all display a number of characteristics from a long list of those appropriate to the family.

Judgement is needed to avoid such classifications as Plato's of man as a featherless biped. In fact, man is now seen to be much more closely related to most quadrupeds, and to dolphins which appear to have no feet at all. Aristotle saw this latter distinction. He referred to homologues where organs similar in structure play different roles (e.g. human feet and dolphins' flippers), and to analogues, where similar functions are performed by quite different organs (e.g. birds' wings and bees' wings). It is the homologues which indicate nearness. This concept will be returned to later.

When different species are observed or measured, the various characteristics need to be weighted by the taxonomist. Without weighting, the 'convergence' or analogues mentioned in the above paragraph might lead to misclassification. A classification without weighting is called phenetic (based on appearances); one involving weighting is phyletic. In effect, biologists concentrate heavily on a genetic or developmental form of classification. Where the fossil record is adequate, classification is fairly easy; where it is not, phyletic classification is used as a substitute.

Judgement is particularly obvious, too, when one notes the changes of mind which have been necessary this century in order to allow for bacteria, blue-green algae and various other borderline problems. It was not even clear where 'animal' stopped and 'plant' began. Thus new categories were invented, and five-kingdom or four-kingdom classifications rather than a two-kingdom classification are now used. However, the borderline 'problem' has been recognized in effect not to be a problem, but an inevitable concomitant of accepting that one species gradually evolves from another.

David and Brierley (1978), who have classified legal systems, warn us that, for social sciences, there are similar subtleties. Their words are of such great relevance to accounting classification (as will become clear in chapter 5) that a substantial quotation is here included:

> the diversity of laws does not really reside in the fact that different national laws may on a variety of topics have different rules. . . . The law of any country will, of course, be concretely manifested at any given time by means of just such a series of rules – the juridical phenomenon which they represent is, however, far more complex. Each law in fact constitutes a *system*. . . .
> When endeavouring to determine the families into which different laws can be grouped, it is preferable to take into consideration these constant elements rather than the less stable rules found in the law at any given moment. . . . The classification of laws into families should not be made on the basis of the similarity or dissimilarity of any particular legal rules, important as they may be; this is . . . inappropriate when highlighting what is truly significant in the characteristics of a given system of law.
>
> (18–19)

Thus, a classification is by no means theory-free. A sensible classification is not produced by a summarization of a mass of facts. It involves preconceptions, judgements and weightings. Taxonomy is a matter of interpretation: finding the homologues. Thus, when the present author attempts a classification in a later chapter, he begins with an hypothesis about how accounting systems are classified.

Desiderata

Some proposed rules of classification have been summarized by the American Accounting Association (1977: 77–8). Drawing on set theory, four properties were seen as useful. First, the characteristics of a classification should be adhered to consistently. That is, through-out any classification the characteristics used as the means of differentiating one element from another should be the same. If it is the number of feet of an animal, then this should be adhered to. However, different purposes for a classification may of course lead to the use of different characteristics, and in practice it may turn out to be impractical to obey this criterion.

Second, a good classification should contain sufficient subsets to exhaust a given universe. That is, a chemical element, or a plant, or an accounting system should not be unclassifiable due to possessing an extreme amount of a characteristic or to displaying no character-istics which are criteria for classification in the system.

Third, all subsets should be mutually exclusive in such a way that no element may fall into more than one of them. (The discovery of a duck-billed platypus, which lays eggs but suckles its young, neces-sitates a new group labelled 'monotremes'.) As has been said, recogni-tion of evolution casts some doubt on the practicality of this criterion.

Lastly, hierarchical integrity should be observed. For example, in the Linnaean biological classification, any species of plant or animal is always in the bottom tier of the main ranks of the classification (except, that is, for individuals within a species), always belongs to a *genus*, which belongs to a *family*, and so on, as in table 3.2.

EXAMPLES OF CLASSIFICATION

Before looking at international comparative accounting classifica-tions, it may be useful to examine classifications in other fields.

Languages

Classification of languages is a fascinating field, bearing some resemb-lances to biology. It gradually came to be recognized that there was a family of Indo-European languages during the eighteenth century, particularly after the study of Sanskrit. The idea that all these languages came from a common prehistoric source seems first to have been stated in 1786 by a Sanskrit scholar, Sir William Jones. Classification within the family proceeded throughout the nineteenth century, starting with a treatise on inflexional endings in Sanskrit, Greek, Latin, Persian and Germanic in 1816 by Franz Bopp. Table 3.3 shows similarities in basic words for some of the languages in the Indo-European family. Appendix IV shows a broad classification of many of the world's existing languages.

Table 3.3 Indo-European languages

English	mother	two	three	is
Sanskrit	mātā	dvau	trayah	asti
Greek	mētēr	duo	treis	esti
Latin	mater	duo	trēs	est
French	mère	deux	trois	est
Italian	madre	due	tre	e
German	Mutter	zwei	drei	ist
Russian	mat'	dva	tri	jest'

Note: Dutch, Danish, Swedish, Polish, Serbian and Spanish all fit in with this table. Even less closely related languages like Persian, Welsh and Armenian fit well.

As in biology, classification is in effect performed on a genetic or heredity basis. In the case of the Romance languages the 'fossil record' is extremely clear in the preservation of Latin and vulgar forms of it down through the centuries. In the case of Germanic languages, the record is not so clear, so a 'primitive Germanic' is postulated and study is made instead of common inflexions, pronunciations, basic vocabulary and so on (Bloomfield 1935).

Political systems

Political systems were grouped by Aristotle into three forms of government, using as a first factor the number and wealth of those who held formal authority in the state. Then he subdivided these categories according to whether those who held authority were concerned with community or private well-being. Thus he arrived at monarchy–tyranny, aristocracy–oligarchy, *politeia*–democracy. He further subdivided: for example, monarchy is split into five types.

A great deal more recently, political systems have been grouped into political democracies, tutelary democracies, modernizing oligarchies, totalitarian oligarchies and traditional oligarchies (Shils 1966). More attempts have been made, like Aristotle's, to use morphologies to help with political classification, as table 3.4 shows. This can be carried considerably further as shown in figure 3.2, which could be used for clustering. Such classification activity is abundant in comparative politics; another example is shown in figure 3.3.

Economies

Economic systems have been divided into capitalism, socialism, communism and fascism; or into traditional economies, market

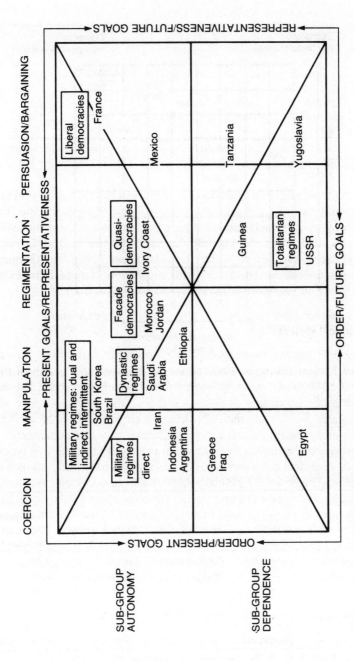

Figure 3.2 A political clustering
Source: As table 3.4

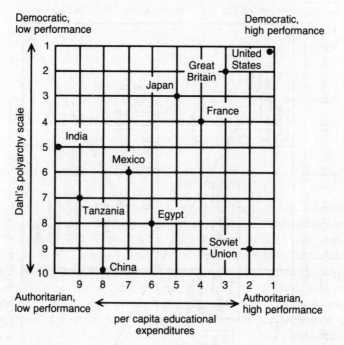

Figure 3.3 Selected nations ranked by political competitiveness and performance
Source: Almond, G. A. *Comparative Politics Today*, Boston: Little, Brown and Co.: 28
Note: The indicator of performance is per capita governmental expenditure on education.

Table 3.4 A political morphology on two factors

	Coercion (Fear)	Manipulation (Deference)	Regimentation (Sentiments)	Persuasion/ Bargaining (Cognition/ Interests)
Participation	Indonesia	Afghanistan Iran	Mexico Tanzania	USA UK France
Exclusion	Iraq Burma Argentina	Saudi-Arabia	Albania USSR	

Source: Finer, S. E. (1970) *Comparative Government*, Penguin: 45

Table 3.5 Economic systems classification

Family	Species	
Tradition		Traditional
Market	Decentralized	Perfectly competitive market
		Imperfectly competitive market
	Centralized	Oscar Lange model I
		Central market survey
Planned market		Indicative planning
		Visible hand
Plan	Decentralized	Oscar Lange model II
	Centralized	Oscar Lange model III
		Centralized command
		Centralized solidarity

Source: Neuberger and Duffy (1976): 103

economies and planned economics. Somewhat greater detail has also been attempted (see table 3.5).

One pair of classifiers of economic systems has identified four fundamental differentiating factors and gone on to construct a type of morphology based on this (Gregory and Stuart 1980). The four factors are decision-making structure, mechanisms for information and co-ordination, property rights and incentives. The morphology is shown in figure 3.4 and implies a three-group classification.

	Capitalism	*Market socialism*	*Planned socialism*
Decision-making structure	primarily decentralized	primarily decentralized	primarily centralized
Mechanisms for information	primarily market	primarily market	primarily plan
Property rights	primarily private ownership	state and/or collective ownership	primarily state ownership
Incentives	primarily material	material and moral	material and moral

Figure 3.4 Economic systems classification morphology
Source: Gregory and Stewart (1980)

Legal systems

Legal systems have also been classified (Kagan 1955). David and Brierley (1978) have produced a four-group classification: Romano-Germanic, Common Law, Socialist and Philosophical–Religious. The latter authors mention two criteria for determining whether two systems are in the same group (1978: 20). Systems are said to be in the same group if 'someone educated in ... one law will then be capable, without much difficulty, of handling (the other)'. This is somewhat vague and more useful for such a four-group classification than for a more detailed one. However, it might be regarded as a necessary condition for two systems to be of the same 'species'. For example, on this basis, the English spoken in the UK and the USA may be said to be of the same 'species'. The definition may also suggest that the accounting practices of those countries are also within the same 'species'.

The second criterion is that the two systems must not be 'founded on opposed philosophical, political or economic principles'. This would ensure that systems in the same group not only have similar superficial characteristics, but also have similar fundamental structures and influences on development, and are likely to react to new circumstances in similar ways. It should help to guard against classifying *homo sapiens* as a featherless biped.

Conclusion

All the social science classifications have been rudimentary, involving no more than splitting systems into a few groups, which are perhaps not precisely defined or exhaustive. Also the method of classification was clearly subjective and based on personal knowledge and descriptive literature. These 'shortcomings' are difficult to avoid because of the complexity and 'greyness' in social sciences. Further, to repeat an earlier point, useful classification is bound to be subjective. Even in a science like biology, somebody has to decide which characteristics to measure, how to weight them (even if it is only to decide to give them all equal weight), and then these characteristics have to be measured. A more detailed consideration of the need for theory and the dangers of 'empiricism' are discussed in chapter 5.

4 Classification in accounting

To make such a comparison as is called for by the title of this paper implies first of all, exact knowledge as to what is the accounting practice of any particular country. But who can with confidence describe even the practice of American railways in regard to showing sinking fund transactions?

Hatfield, H. R. (reprinted 1966)

EARLY CLASSIFICATIONS AND RECENT DATA

The paper by Hatfield of 1911 (quoted above) may serve as a background to more recent comparative accounting classifications. He discussed the accounting practices in the UK, USA, France and Germany. He frequently notes the similarities, on the one hand between the UK and the USA, and on the other hand between France and Germany. However, he does conclude with a classification into UK, US and continental. This perhaps shows that he knew UK and US accounting better, and was thus more aware of their differences.

There are also descriptions of the development of accounting in various countries by Zeff (1972) and by Nobes and Parker (1979). Descriptions of practices are referred to in chapters 2 and 3 of the present work. Further, there are international surveys of practice by Price Waterhouse (1973, 1976–9), the AICPA (1964, 1975), the OECD (1980) and Gray *et al.* (1984). These provide a mass of data which may be used for classification.

Mueller's classifications

In the late 1960s, Professor Gerhard Mueller broke new ground by preparing suggested classifications of accounting systems (1967) and of business environments (1968). His classification of accounting systems into four patterns of development is a simple grouping which is not accompanied by an explanation of the methods used to obtain it. However, the 'range of four is considered sufficient to embrace accounting as it is presently known and practised in various parts of the globe' (Mueller 1968: 2). Each group is illustrated by one or two examples. It may well be that it is not reasonable to expect a more sophisticated classification, particularly in a pioneering work, and that Mueller's informed judgement was one of the best methods of classification available.

Mueller stresses that the types of accounting rules which exist in a country are a product of economic, political and other environments, which have determined the nature of the system. This also suggests that other countries' rules would not be appropriate to that country and that rules must be chosen to fit a country's needs. Consequently, doubt is cast on the possibility and usefulness of harmonization.

Mueller's four groups, which are summarized in a later work (Choi and Mueller 1978: ch. 2), are:

1 Accounting within a macroeconomic framework

In this case, accounting has developed as an adjunct of national economic policies. We might expect such financial accounting to stress value-added statements, to encourage income-smoothing, to be equivalent to tax accounting and to include social responsibility accounting. Sweden is said to be an example.

2 The microeconomic approach

This approach can prosper in a market-oriented economy which has individual private businesses at the core of its economic affairs. The influence of microeconomics has led accounting to try to reflect economic reality in its measurements and valuations. This means that accounting rules must be sophisticated, but flexible. Developments like replacement cost accounting will be accepted most readily in such systems. The Netherlands is suggested as an example.

3 Accounting as an independent discipline

Systems of this sort have developed independently of governments or economic theories. Accounting has developed in business, has faced problems when they arrived and has adopted solutions which worked.

Theory is held in little regard and turned to only in emergencies or used *ex post* in an attempt to justify practical conclusions. Expressions such as 'generally accepted accounting principles' are typical. Mueller recognizes the accounting systems of the United Kingdom and the United States as examples. He is clearly making a similar point, though many years before and for a quite different reason, to Watts and Zimmerman (1979) when they argue that 'no normative theory currently in the accounting literature . . . can explain or will be used to justify all accounting standards'. It has also been said that accountancy is 'patron based' and subservient to business interests rather than to theory (Johnson 1972: 71–4).

4 Uniform accounting

Such systems have developed where governments have used accounting as a part of the administrative control of business. Accounting can be used to measure performance, allocate funds, assess the size of industries and resources, control prices, collect taxation, manipulate sectors of business and so on. It involves standardization of definitions, measurements and presentations. France is cited as an example.

Mueller was not classifying accounting systems directly, but on the basis of differences in the importance of economic, governmental and business factors in the development of particular systems. However, one might expect that systems which have developed in a similar way would have similar accounting practices. Chapter 2 suggests that the UK and the USA have similar accounting practices; Mueller's developmental classification also puts them together.

Nevertheless, there are a few problems with Mueller's classification. The fact that there are only four exclusive groups and no hierarchy reduces the usefulness of the classification. Thus, the Netherlands is the only country in one of the groups, and the classification does not show whether Dutch accounting is closer to Anglo-Saxon accounting that it is to Swedish accounting. Similarly, the classification cannot include such facts as that German accounting exhibits features which remind one of macroeconomic accounting as well as uniform accounting. Lastly, Russian or Communistic accounting is left out entirely. This may, of course, be sensible if the classification is dealing with published financial reporting (see p. 63).

As has been said, the strengths of Mueller's classifications are its pioneering nature and that it considers the context and development

Table 4.1 Business environment classification

Factors:
1 Stages of economic development
2 Stages of business complexity
3 Shades of political persuasion
4 Reliance on some particular system of law
Sets of environments:
1 United States/Canada/The Netherlands
2 British Commonwealth (excluding Canada)
3 Germany/Japan
4 Continental Europe (excluding Germany, Netherlands, Scandinavia)
5 Scandinavia
6 Israel/Mexico
7 South America
8 The developing nations of Near and Far East
9 Africa (excluding South Africa)
10 Communist nations

Source: Mueller, G. G. (1968): 92–5

of accounting systems. Thus, it does not make the mistake of misclassification based on superficial similarities.

Mueller's (1968) second classification is of business environments. He again makes his point that different business environments need different accounting systems and that this should be considered when trying to change or harmonize accounting. Mueller uses estimates of economic development, business complexity, legal system and political and social climate. Ten groupings are identified (see table 4.1). Although the group comprising 'developing nations of the Near and Far East' might be argued to *need* similar accounting systems, it surely does not have them. Further, the 'Israel and Mexico' group is perhaps an example of man as a featherless biped or of David and Brierley's second criterion being broken. That is, although these countries may have appeared similar at one moment, they have different underlying political, social, geographical, religious and historical factors. Thus, to expect them to continue to react in a similar way for the purposes of accounting or business is to invite disappointment.

MORPHOLOGIES

It was noted in the previous chapter that a morphology may help one towards a classification. The stage before a morphology is a one-dimensional list of characteristics deemed relevant for classification. For example, Previts (1975) provides a list of environmental conditions:

Table 4.2 The AAA's morphology for comparative accounting systems

Parameters			States of nature		
	1	*2*	*3*	*4*	*5*
P$_1$ Political system	Traditional oligarchy	Totalitarian oligarchy	Modernizing oligarchy	Tutelary democracy	Political democracy
P$_2$ Economic system	Traditional	Market	Planned market	Plan	
P$_3$ Stages of economic development	Traditional society	Pre-take-off	Take-off	Drive to maturity	Mass consumption
			Micro		Macro
P$_4$ Objectives of financial reporting	Investment decisions	Management performance	Social measurement	Sector planning and control	National policy objective
P$_5$ Source of, or authority for standards	Executive degree	Legislative action	Government administrative unit	Public–private consortium	Private
			Public	Private	
P$_6$ Education, training and licensing	Informal	Formal	Informal	Formal	
P$_7$ Enforcement of ethics and standards	Executive	Government administrative unit	Judicial	Private	
P$_8$ Client	Government	Public	Enterprises		
			Public	Private	

Source: Accounting Review Supplement to Vol. 52 (1977) American Accounting Association: 99

1 stability of currency;
2 nature of business ownership;
3 level of management sophistication;
4 size and complexity of businesses;
5 speed of technological and commercial innovation;
6 presence of specific accounting legislation;
7 type of economy and degree of market freedom;
8 growth pattern of the economy;
9 status of accounting education;
10 status of accounting profession;
11 general level of public education;
12 extent of kindred financial knowledge which would require the existence of sophisticated financial reports to the community; and
13 legal and customary structures of business and finance.

A morphology would need at least one more dimension (AAA 1977: 82). For example, that of the American Accounting Association is shown in table 4.2. Another, by the Buckleys (1974) concerns the method of setting accounting rules, but was not proposed directly for international purposes. It is shown as table 4.3. Such parameters as the first two of table 4.2 (political and economic systems) may seem less relevant than actual characteristics of accounting practice. However, one should remember David and Brierley's warning about the importance of underlying structure as opposed to transitory detail. Inclusion of such background factors may help to avoid the 'Israel with Mexico' problem. The AAA's (1977: 97) Committee on International Accounting notes that, 'Parameters P1 and P2 are viewed as being pivotal to the type of accounting system which does (or can) emerge'.

Table 4.3 A morphology for establishing accounting standards

Parameters	1	2	3	4	5
A Principal beneficiary	Government/ public sector	Investors/ analysts	Capital/ credit markets	Management	Accountants
B Climate	Laissez-faire	Uniformity	Circumstantial variables	–	–
C Rationale	Inductive theoretic	Deductive theoretic	Pragmatic	Authoritarian	Plebiscite (poll)
D Where authority vests	Private- accounting profession	Private- consortium	Public (government)	Quasi-public	–
E Primary objective	Conformity	Curb abuses	Power	Authority	Abstract- theoretic
F Sociological rationale	Public- protection	Public service	Private rights	Profession's welfare	–
G Impetus	Internal	Regulatory	Societal	–	–

Source: Buckley, J. W. and M. H. (1974) *The Accounting Profession*, Melville, Los Angeles: 139

These two morphologies have not been taken further to produce a classification of similar countries into groups. It is worth noting just how they fit in with the previous discussion on the techniques of classification. The eight parameters in table 4.2 are an assessment of the most important structural elements in accounting systems. Thus they are to be used as a means of differentiating between systems. The other two stages of judgement involved in classification would be the assignment of weights to these factors, and then the measurement of each country on each of the parameters.

Mueller's classifications and the 'spheres of influence' classifications discussed immediately below have not made such parameters explicit, but by implication they must have been (at least subconsciously) present. The classifications produced using a computer in conjunction with a mass of data from surveys like that of Price Waterhouse have, in effect, generated all three stages from the data. Although such classifications may seem more scientific, they may actually contain a fundamental flaw. This is discussed in chapter 5, p. 55.

SPHERES OF INFLUENCE

There have been some further 'subjective' classifications based on 'spheres of influence'. Seidler (1967) suggested three groups: British, American and continental European. Also, although the AAA's committee (1977: 105, 129–30) did not take its morphology further, it did produce a 'zones of influence' classification. The zones are:

1 British
2 Franco-Spanish-Portuguese
3 Germanic-Dutch
4 US
5 Communistic

These zones might equally well have been produced by an historian or a politician. This is not, of course, necessarily a criticism, bearing in mind the importance of context and development to a proper classification. This classification may be useful when examining the accounting practices of developing countries. However, it seems not to be an advance on Mueller's first classification. It adds no hierarchy, for example. Furthermore, it does not take account of the links between UK and US accounting, yet it groups Germanic with Dutch. This seems inappropriate in the light of the material summarized in chapter 2, and certainly runs counter to Mueller's classification.

5 Statistical classifications

Although accounting as an academic subject has been relatively recently established, the developments reviewed in the previous chapter suggest that international comparative classification has come at least as far in accounting as in other social sciences. In the late 1970s and early 1980s there was an intensification of activity in this area, which appears to have taken classification in accounting well beyond that of the other disciplines mentioned in chapter 3. At least four independent researchers were progressing with similar work. For some time, the present author was not aware of the work of others which had been completed but not published. The published work of three groups of researchers is looked at in this chapter; the present author's results are set out in the next.

Before examining these works on classification, from which ideas may be gleaned and lessons learned, their common methodology is discussed.

GENERAL DESCRIPTION OF METHODOLOGY

All the researchers referred to later in this chapter have attempted to produce classifications by using Price Waterhouse survey data. This comprises information on over two hundred accounting practices relating to a number of countries. These are scored on an ordinal scale (e.g. from 0 to 5). There have been three surveys, all of which have been used by at least one researcher. The size of the surveys is shown in table 5.1. An example of scoring on a practice is shown in table 5.2.

The Price Waterhouse data were used by each of the researchers as input to various statistical processes, including factor analysis and cluster analysis. The former process involves the identification of factors which explain the variance between the countries. These

Table 5.1 Dimensions of Price Waterhouse surveys

	1973	1976	1979
Number of countries	38	46	64
Number of practices	233	264	267
Length of scale	6	7	7

'factors' are selections of practices with different weights which best explain the variance. It may be possible to assign descriptions to these factors by noting the flavour of the mixture of practices in the factors. As will be seen, some researchers have thus been able to label their factors.

The next stage is that a certain number of the most explanatory factors is selected. Then, the 'significant' scores or all the scores on the relevant practices making up the factors are used to calculate the correlations of each country on each factor. It is hoped that clusters of countries will thereby emerge.

The reason why some researchers have taken only some factors and only 'significant' scores is that they believe that the resulting greater clarity justifies the loss of some information.

'EMPIRICAL' CLASSIFIERS

Da Costa, Bourgeois and Lawson (DBL)

The earliest published study to be included here is by Da Costa, Bourgeois and Lawson (1978). They used the 1973 Price Waterhouse data which scores 38 countries on 233 accounting practices. DBL, however, use only 100 of these, claiming that 'the data base was screened to eliminate practices which were uniform across countries'. Inspection of the survey reveals only three entirely uniform practices. It is perhaps worth noting that the factor analysis section of the SPSS computer package which they were using accepts a maximum of 100 variables (Nie *et al.* 1974).

The first stage of DBL's analysis found seven independent factors which explained 63 per cent of the sum of the variances of the scores on each practice. A score was then computed for each country on those seven factors for each practice with which the factor showed a 'significant' correlation. The countries were then correlated with each other and a 'Q-analysis' was performed using the correlation matrix. In such analyses, if one or more countries has a high correlation with one factor and with no other then they may reasonably be grouped into a cluster.

Table 5.2 Practice 93 'Inventories', Price Waterhouse 1975

	6	5	4	3	2	1	0
Argentina				*			
Australia		*					
Bahamas		*					
Belgium		*					
Bermuda		*					
Bolivia				*			
Brazil				*			
Canada			*				
Chile						*	
Colombia			*				
Denmark		*					
Ethiopia		*					
Fiji		*					
France			*				
Germany				*			
Greece				*			
India				*			
Iran				*			
Italy				*			
Jamaica		*					
Japan				*			
Kenya			*				
Malaysia		*					
Mexico				*			
Netherlands		*					
New Zealand		*					
Nigeria			*				
Norway			*				
Pakistan			*				
Panama		*					
Paraguay				*			
Peru			*				
Philippines		*					
Rep of Ireland		*					
Rhodesia			*				
Singapore		*					
South Africa			*				
Spain		*					
Sweden		*					
Switzerland			*				
Trinidad		*					
United Kingdom	*						
United States		*					
Uruguay				*			
Venezuela			*				
Zaire				*			

Note:
Cost determined using FIFO.
0 = no application
1 = not permitted
2 = not found in
 practice
3 = minority
4 = about half
5 = majority
6 = required

The seven factors found by DBL were examined and found to consist of 'recipes' of practices which would be described as follows:

1 Degree of financial disclosure
2 Influence of company law on accounting practice
3 Importance of income measurement
4 Strength of conservatism
5 Influence of tax laws
6 Importance of inflation in the environment
7 Orientation towards capital market users

These factors seem very reasonable as measures of some of the structural differences between the accounting systems of different countries. The clustering process which followed produced two groups (see table 5.3). One group contained the UK and nine former members of the British Empire. The other group contained the USA, France, Germany, South American countries and all others except the Netherlands and Canada which were said to be unclassifiable.

At this point, common sense might have intervened and cast doubt on the meaning of a group containing the US and Germany but not Canada. It is not a great surprise that, if one has only two groups and they are headed by the UK and the USA, then Canada will be difficult to classify. However, is 'group 1' a sensible group? Ignoring the Canadian point for the moment, does it enhance our understanding of comparative accounting to have the USA in the same group as Ethiopia but not as the UK? Surely, the paper's conclusion should have been that it had been useful to test the database, that results had been obtained but that something must be wrong with the data or the methodology, or that more stages to the work were needed before it could be usefully interpreted.

However, there was no such caution. The US was said to be 'the country most dissociated from the British model' (80), following on from the remarkable (but apparently believed) co-efficient of 0.05 shown in the right-hand column of table 5.3 which suggests that of all the countries in the survey, US accounting is much the least like UK accounting. Further, it was concluded that the group containing France, Germany, etc., 'follows the lead of the United States in dissociating themselves from practices common to the British model' (83). It seems highly unlikely that the makers of company and tax laws that govern accounting in France, Germany, Belgium and Italy bear in mind either that they should follow the USA or that they should dissociate themselves from the UK when legislating.

This paper was pioneering and interesting, but it does present an

Table 5.3 Countries grouped on the basis of the association among their financial accounting practices

Countries	Co-efficient with	
	Group 1	Group 2
Group 1; nc = 26		
Japan	0.95	0.28
Philippines	0.94	0.28
Mexico	0.93	0.32
Argentina	0.93	0.32
Germany	0.90	0.42
Chile	0.90	0.41
Bolivia	0.89	0.43
Panama	0.89	0.45
Italy	0.88	0.43
Peru	0.88	0.43
Venezuela	0.88	0.46
Colombia	0.86	0.50
Paraguay	0.86	0.48
United States	0.86	0.05
Pakistan	0.85	0.49
Spain	0.85	0.49
Switzerland	0.84	0.53
Brazil	0.83	0.51
France	0.83	0.53
Uruguay	0.82	0.52
Sweden	0.81	0.59
India	0.81	0.57
Ethiopia	0.81	0.57
Belgium	0.79	0.60
Trinidad	0.76	0.65
Bahamas	0.75	0.65
Group 2; nc = 10		
United Kingdom	0.004	0.98
Eire	0.19	0.96
Rhodesia	0.48	0.87
Singapore	0.50	0.86
South Africa	0.51	0.86
Australia	0.51	0.85
Jamaica	0.54	0.84
Kenya	0.57	0.81
New Zealand	0.62	0.78
Fiji	0.65	0.75

Source: da Costa *et al.* (1978): 79

excellent illustration of many of the problems which are discussed in the later sections of this chapter.

Frank

Frank's (1979) paper uses the same data as DBL, performs a broadly similar analysis, and then adds a study of whether the results fit with social and economic environmental factors. Frank identifies four groups, as shown in table 5.4. He cautions us that certain countries bear strong affinities with groups other than their own, and he checks the results with 'multi-dimensional scaling'. This latter technique avoids the problem which may follow from the 'categorical' scoring. It counts the number of times the scores on practices are the same for each possible pair of countries.

Table 5.4 Four-group classification (Frank) 1973 data

Group I	Group II	Group III	Group IV
Australia	Argentina	Belgium	Canada
Bahamas	Bolivia	Colombia	Germany
Ethiopia	Brazil	France	Japan
Eire	Chile	Italy	Mexico
Fiji	India	Spain	Netherlands
Jamaica	Pakistan	Sweden	Panama
Kenya	Paraguay	Switzerland	Philippines
New Zealand	Peru	Venezuela	United States
Rhodesia	Uruguay		
Singapore			
South Africa			
Trinidad and Tobago			
United Kingdom			

Source: Frank (1979): 596

Frank is much more careful than DBL when discussing whether his results are 'correct' or suggesting that previous subjective classifications may be wrong. However, he clearly feels that such 'empirical' work is an advance on previous subjectivity, without being concerned with the subjectively collected 'empirical' data. He does not discuss the fact that physical and life scientists do not classify in this way. They judge which factors are structural, and use only measurements of these factors for the differentiation which leads to classification.

Nevertheless, it must be said that the four-group result looks very sensible compared to the DBL results. In effect, this comes from splitting down DBL's Group I. No doubt this involved the use of a considerable amount of judgement at various stages of the analysis; this is clearly an essential element but one which the various researchers seem rather ashamed of. However, one might still feel concerned about grouping the USA with Germany and Japan, and not with the UK. In a later work involving Frank (discussed below) this problem is resolved by usefully recognizing that *disclosure* practices and *measurement* practices are interfering with each other and need to be separated.

Frank's analysis of social, cultural and economic factors generally supports his four-group classification. It supports ideas that 'cultural and economic factors are associated with the particular set of accounting principles and practices used by various countries' (604).

Nair and Frank

Perhaps the most attractive results, as far as concerns those factors which the present author considers as fundamental and structural, are those of Nair and Frank (1980) when dealing with accounting measurement practices. In this paper, the exercise of judgement is seen more clearly. Both the 1973 and the 1975 surveys are used, but split into those practices concerned with disclosure and those with measurement. This decision, and the resulting difference in the groups, strongly confirms the point that Price Waterhouse's subjectivity in choosing the questions is a vital factor to be considered when processing the data. The 1973 groupings on measurement practices are shown in table 5.5.

These groupings were produced by using a varimax rotation procedure with the five factors which explained most of the variance (those with eigenvalues exceeding 1.0, explaining 71 per cent of the variance between them).[1] This procedure associates each country with a single factor. No country had its highest loading on the fifth factor.

What clearly emerge are four very plausible groups. These bear a similarity to those of Frank using the whole 1973 survey. However, the differences between them (compare tables 5.4 and 5.5) are very interesting. The Netherlands has moved into the UK group which, apart from the former's experimentation with replacement cost and even more 'judgemental' accounting, seems quite reasonable. Germany has moved into a continental European group, leaving behind a US group which is now very credible. Germany's detailed disclosure requirements are no longer confused with its measurement practices, which are importantly different from those of the USA.

Table 5.5 Four-group 'measurement' classification, Nair and Frank (1973)

Group I	Group II	Group III	Group IV
Australia	Argentina	Belgium	Canada
Bahamas	Bolivia	France	Japan
Fiji	Brazil	Germany	Mexico
Jamaica	Chile	Italy	Panama
Kenya	Colombia	Spain	Philippines
Netherlands	Ethiopia	Sweden	United States
New Zealand	India	Switzerland	
Pakistan	Paraguay	Venezuela	
Republic of Ireland	Peru		
Rhodesia	Uruguay		
Singapore			
South Africa			
Trinidad and Tobago			
United Kingdom			

Source: Nair and Frank (1980): 429

Group II contains mostly South American countries, many of which have adopted some form of general purchasing power accounting.

These results were found to be stable by using the 1975 data. Only a few countries change their groups. This could have been a result of adding extra countries, or of a real change in the accounting practices of these few countries. In the case of Venezuela, which moves from Group III to Group IV, it seems plausible that increasing industrial development and influence of multinational companies explains this. In the case of Pakistan, which moves from Group I to Group II, important political and social changes in the 1970s may explain this. These two countries were noticed in the same way by the present writer in a paper given before Nair and Frank's was published.[2]

As in Frank's 1979 paper, the social and environmental tests are performed, this time on the 1975 data. Similar supporting evidence about their importance is found.

As for the classification of disclosure practices, it is noted that 'the disclosure practices do not seem to conform to any such conceptual classification schemes. They present a different picture of greater diversity where the boundary lines between different groups become blurred and indistinct.'

For measurement practices, with which the writer is more concerned, table 5.5 represents a most attractive result. It suggests that, despite all the fears, the data and the methodology are good enough. Perhaps Price Waterhouse turn out to have asked the questions which do reveal the underlying measurement practices, once the interference from the disclosure practices has been removed. Perhaps any 'hard' errors are unbiased and unimportant. Also, too, it seems likely that Nair and Frank used considerable judgement in the exact methods of choosing groups. They note that their results are 'intuitively appealing' (429), giving the game away that they did expect or hope to confirm the ideas of Seidler, Previts and so on (see ch. 4) whom they begin with.

Despite this, they still make a statement which might be considered to overplay their hand when they describe the research as 'aimed at empirically assessing the validity of international classifications proposed repeatedly in the accounting literature' (449). It is really we and those earlier researchers (and, I suspect, Nair and Frank) who assess the validity of this new classification in the light of our feeling for the underlying structures in comparative accounting. To some extent they do acknowledge this by noting that:

> Since the affiliation of a given country with others is dependent upon the set of accounting practices selected, the validity of cross-country comparisons depends upon the nature of the practice on which the comparison is made.

(449)

Here they were particularly referring to the difference between the measurement and the disclosure subjects, but it must of course also apply to the difference between the Price Waterhouse survey and any possible Arthur Andersen, etc, survey. That being the case, the usefulness of the Price Waterhouse survey is not that it avoids subjectivity but that it has already been carried out. It would be just as empirical and far more relevant (but much more time consuming) to judge which factors are important for differentiation and to go out and measure them personally in each country.

A real empirical *test* of the classification, as opposed to the *generation* of it, might be to study whether the four different groups react in four different internally homogeneous ways to certain stimuli, such as rapid inflation.

Goodrich

Goodrich (1982) uses the Price Waterhouse (1979) survey data and factor analysis. He detects five groupings, each headed by a prototype country: USA, Switzerland, UK, Brazil and Jersey. The Jersey group contains Germany, the Netherlands, Italy, Senegal and Ecuador. The fact that Goodrich takes such a group seriously (57) is the best illustration imaginable of the pitfalls of the 'empirical' method. As

Nobes (1982) points out, it is hard to take seriously a classification that puts Australia in the same group as Japan and Columbia, and not with the UK and New Zealand. Further discussion followed in Goodrich (1983) and Nobes (1983).

CRITICISM OF THE 'EMPIRICAL' CLASSIFICATIONS' SCORING METHOD

One may criticize both the methodology and the data used for the above classifications. The latter is mostly left to the next section. Some of the following methodological criticisms have been discussed by the researchers.

One obvious initial problem is that the Price Waterhouse data are qualitative or categorical. It scores practices by reference to measures like 'minority practice' (see table 5.2). These scores are converted by the researchers into either percentages or ordinal scores, designed to represent the mid-point of intervals or indicators of a range of values of an underlying continuous scale. Compared with the other problems mentioned in this and the following sections, this scoring problem does not seem too serious. One of the researchers has carried out an assessment of the error and regards it as unimportant (Nair and Frank 1980: 445).

The need for an hypothesis

A more serious problem relates to the nature and purpose of classification. It has been suggested in the preceding two chapters (particularly chapter 3, p. 32) that sensible classification cannot be theory-free; that statistical analysis should be used to test, not to generate, hypotheses (Armstrong 1967). Further, discussion has been entered into about the importance of underlying structures as opposed to outward and visible forms. All these points seem not to have been properly taken into account by the researchers studied above.

One must know exactly what is being classified and for what purpose. One must study the data to see if it measures practices relevant to this. Further, one must ensure that the differentiation between countries is carried out on the basis of important structural variables. To use cluster analysis on the raw Price Waterhouse data with no prior theoretical input will merely show how the Price Waterhouse data may be clustered. It will not show how to classify, for example, the various national systems of accounting measurement practices used by listed companies in developed Western nations.

Suppose that a German firm of pet shops called, shall we say, Preis und Wasserhaus measures a number of different animals on the following characteristics: weight, number of legs, colour, life expectancy, preferred habitat, geographical spread, popularity with customers, type of food consumed, etc. Their survey is concerned with the analysis of the best pets to keep in stock. Later, an academic biologist uses this survey to attempt a classification of the animals covered (plus *homo sapiens*). He does so because the data have not been corrupted by his own preconceptions of which factors are important in classifications, and how particular animals should be scored.

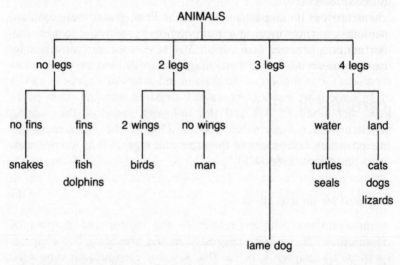

Figure 5.1 Classification of animals based on the Preis und Wasserhaus survey

The initial results, somewhat at variance with a Linnaean classification, might be as found in figure 5.1. This shows the splitting of the animals in the sample based on the most powerfully differentiating factor for the characteristics measured, which turn out to be strongly associated with the number of legs. At this preliminary stage, conventional biology might put seals, dolphins, man, cats and dogs (of however many legs) together on the basis of method of reproduction and allied matters. It would turn out, too, that such a grouping might have behavioural and neurological similarities. However, these were omitted from the survey, because to some extent they were difficult to measure and to some extent they were of no interest to Preis und Wasserhaus.

The classification in figure 5.1 might then be used to challenge conventional, subjective, non-statistical, non-empirical views.

The moral of this story may be in some ways unattractive to 'scientific' researchers. It is that it may be useful to start with an hypothesis of how the universe looks, to judge which factors are important as fundamental discriminators, to have in mind a purpose for the classification, and so on. This does not mean that a database is of no use, but it does mean that judgement must be used. The empirical researcher may regret the need to 'tamper' with data. However, why should we believe, for example, that the subjective selection of characteristics by Price Waterhouse for quite another purpose than classification is any better than a subjective selection of characteristics by a researcher for his own purposes? Why should a subjective scoring on any particular characteristic by a busy practising partner be any better than a subjective scoring by well-informed and careful researchers?

CRITICISM OF THE DATA

There are several ways in which the *use* of Price Waterhouse data for the purpose of classification might be criticized. There are also some ways in which the data *per se* may be reasonably questioned. The former are clearly not the fault of Price Waterhouse, to whom we should be grateful for the enormous effort involved in compiling this rich source of data. However, taken together, these problems are of great significance, but have not been discussed in any detail by the researchers. They are summarized elsewhere by Nobes (1983).

Suitability for purpose

The 'suitability' point is connected with the previous section. The surveys were not intended as a source of data for classification. They were thus biased towards practical detail rather than fundamental, lasting structure. For example, there are no questions in the surveys designed to establish directly whether accounting is aiming at a 'fair' view, as Anglo-Saxon accountants understand it. This is related to another possible problem, which is that the questions in the survey were chosen by Anglo-Saxon accountants who, being particularly familiar with US and UK accounting, might have set questions which tend to exaggerate the differences between these two countries. The questions may not, thus, fully explore the differences of a more fundamental nature between these and other countries.

Table 5.6 1973 survey questions on consolidation for four countries

Practice no.		US	UK	France	W. Germany
14	Consolidated statements *only*	4	1	2	1
15	Consolidated and parent statements	1	5	2	5
16	Parent statements *only*	1	1	4	1

Note: 1 = not permitted or not found
2 = minority practice
3 = followed by half of companies
4 = majority practice
5 = required

Further, since the computer sees all characteristics as having equal weight, the mix of questions may add an overwhelming background noise to the important theme that some questions may have correctly identified. As an example of this, let us take the three questions on consolidation in the 1973 survey, as shown in table 5.6. There are other questions on goodwill, poolings of interest and associated companies. However, examination of these would merely elaborate the point that the essential difference between the systems is not clearly shown by considering all three questions with equal weight. The vital question is the third, question 16, which separates out France from the other countries shown. Also, the computer might notice that the UK seems to fit with Germany rather than with the USA. This would be misleading, because the computer has not been told that German companies usually excluded foreign subsidiaries and have a different concept of the 'group'. Questions 14 and 15 are of considerable interest to a practitioner but are quite unimportant compared to a more structural question like question 16.

Table 5.7 1973 survey questions on conservatism

Practice no.		US	UK	France	W. Germany
11	Conservatism	5	5	4	5
34	Over-conservative asset valuation	2	1	4	3

Note: Scores as for table 5.6

Misleading cases

There are important examples of scores on practices which may be seen as correct when the context is carefully examined, but which must be misleading when fed into a computer program. Table 5.7

gives the example of conservatism for the four countries in table 5.6. It is true that 'prudence' is enshrined in US and UK accounting statements (APB Statement 4 and SSAP 2). It may also have been true that 'conservatism' was not mentioned in French law as such. Thus, the survey may be 'correct' in its scoring on practice no. 11, by its own definition of the score 'required'. However, the conservatism found in France and Germany is reckoned by those familiar with it to be of a totally different (and higher) order to that used in the USA and the UK. On this fundamental point the computer will be misled. As it turns out, practice no. 34 which is also shown in table 5.7 seems to correspond more with expectations, though there must have been difficulty in standardizing the scoring on over-conservatism, as a German accountant's view might be very different from an English accountant's.

Turning to the 1979 survey (effective date: 1 January 1979), another example of the possibility of being misled is the treatment of international accounting standards and other 'requirements'. Taking consolidation, the survey reports that, for question 209 ('consolidated statements . . . are prepared for the shareholders'), the answer is 'required' in France. The reason given for this is that the *Commission des Opérations de Bourse* (COB) 'requires' consolidation. In fact, as the annual reports of COB show, only 305 companies published consolidated balance sheets and profit and loss accounts in 1979 (see table 2.4). This was less than half of the listed companies (see ch. 2) and a very small proportion of 'enterprises which issue their statements to the general public' about which the survey is said to be (Price Waterhouse 1979: 5).

Further, one wonders whether consolidation practices in Fiji, Malaysia or Trinidad are really correctly understood by suggestions in various survey questions that IAS 3 is being followed. The survey's introduction (8, 9) sounds a note of caution here, but this has not been fed into the computer by the researchers.

These are examples which could be replicated many times over. A related point is made for one particular country by Zeff (1979: 59) who conjectures that 'the Price Waterhouse surveys reported chiefly on the New Zealand subsidiaries of overseas-based corporations, rather than on domestic New Zealand companies'.

Errors

There are examples of what do seem to be 'hard' errors. These are clearly inevitable in a massive undertaking such as one of the

Table 5.8 Survey answers for UK

Practice	Number and score	
	1973	*1976*
A		
'Land is shown separately from other fixed assets'	77 required	40 required
Comment: It was normally unseparated from buildings		
B		
'Cost of inventories is determined by FIFO'		93 required
'Cost of inventories is determined by weighted average'		95 not permitted
'Cost of inventories is determined by retail inventory'		98 not permitted
Comment: SSAP 9 specifically allows all three (appendix, paras 11–14).		
C		
There are several examples where UK practice is said to differ from Irish practice in 1976, yet where the countries used identical standards on the subject, e.g. 205		
D		
'Leases are capitalized by the lessee'	178 majority	47 majority
Comment: This was not the case in 1973 or 1976.		

surveys. Table 5.8 shows some extracts from the 1973 and 1976 surveys relating to the UK. Doubt is thereby cast upon the reliability of anwers for Bolivia!

Conclusion

These problems with the data should reinforce the points in the previous section about the need for judgement and theoretical input. Since the data is not perfect and has not been designed for the work in hand, it should be clear that it needs to be handled with care. Further, the results from using it must be treated with caution. As has been seen in the preceding review of the work of other researchers, it appears that such caution has not always been present.

IMPROVEMENTS SUGGESTED

Let us briefly examine the 'empirical' classifications of an earlier section of this chapter (pp. 48–55) from the point of view of the *desiderata* mentioned in chapter 3.

Consistency

On at least one point it seems clear that the characteristics used for classification are not being held constant in the surveys on which the above researches are based. As Nair and Frank (1980: 445) note 'the companies whose practices are reported on in the survey may not all meet the same criteria such as being listed on a stock exchange, or even being publicly held'. The reverse problem has also been noted earlier in this chapter: for example, that some scores are descriptions of the practice of only important listed companies in some countries but of all companies in other countries (e.g. France and consolidation in the 1979/80 survey). This seems of considerable importance but is difficult to correct for when dealing with a vast mass of characteristics and countries.

Sufficient subsets

To some extent this criterion can be satisfied by definition of the universe in question. In the above research, the number of groups is expanded until there is room to accommodate all the countries. There seems no problem here. Extra countries are added, between 1973 and 1975/6 for example, without serious difficulties.

Mutual exclusivity

Here there are some problems, connected with a lack of detail or hierarchy. The simplicity of a two-group or four-group classification is such that it cannot express the degree to which one country bears features of two different groups – technically, the degree to which one country may have high loading on two or more factors. This was seen, too, in Mueller's classification where France may seem to belong to both the macroeconomic and the uniform accounting group. Further detailed splitting of groups should alleviate this problem.

Hierarchical integrity

With a two-group or four-group model there can hardly be problems
with hierarchical integrity, as there is only one level. The problem
may need to be faced when more detail is added but it should be
easily included.

NOTES

1 Since my own research does not hinge on such methods and since the
  methods are fairly well known, a detailed description is not given here.
  However, Nair and Frank (1980) do discuss this, and there is further
  explanation in Coxon (1982).
2 'Classification of National Systems of Accounting' at AUTA Conference,
  Spring 1980, published as Nobes and Matatko (1980).

6 An hypothesis and some tests of it

This chapter and the one following deal with the present writer's own work in classification.

DEFINITION

In order to improve upon previous classifications, a number of adjustments were attempted. First, for consistency between countries, the scope was limited to accounting as practised by public companies listed on a stock exchange. This initially narrows the universe to developed Western countries and those strongly influenced by them. One problem with this is that the largest of companies in some countries behave very differently from the bulk of companies. For example, although Sweden's accounting is described in the references in appendix I as being a good example of macro-economic or tax-based accounting, its largest companies win international prizes for their financial reports. This seems to be partly because of lavish disclosures and partly because adjustments have been made for the effects of taxation and other differences. In the period under study, Italy was also beginning a fundamental shift towards Anglo-Saxon accounting practices for its listed companies. For Sweden and Italy, the traditional underlying accounting practices are used as the basis of classification here. This may require amendment in subsequent classifications in the future.

A second feature of the classification attempted here is the use of accounting *measurement* practices (rather than disclosure practices, business environments or other matters). Background, context and development are borne in mind and used as a check on the hypothesis, but are not directly included as differentiating variables since they are not accounting practices. Third, the classification relates to 1980, before any substantial harmonizing measures had been introduced by EC member states.

In addition, an attempt is made to satisfy the criteria for good classification discussed in chapter 3. For example, the results introduce a hierarchy, which allows a greater subtlety than is available with, say, a four-group model, where the interrelationships between the groups are not expressed. This also helps to solve the lack of mutual exclusivity that was noted about Mueller's classification and noted by Frank (1979) about his own. That is, it helps to express the degree to which a country's system may belong to one group but show affiliations with another.

As for exhausting the 'universe', having defined it rather narrowly above, exhaustion becomes reasonably practicable. Initially, this is not attempted (see figure 6.1), but the point to note is whether the classification could simply be added to within its existing structure. That is, is the classification as structured, *capable* of exhausting the known universe? Clearly, although the definition above may exclude various developing countries, by relaxing the consistency of definition as to the type of accounting covered, such countries would be included. Here the problem is that it is difficult to extend informed judgement to these countries or to obtain data from sources other than a survey like that of Price Waterhouse. Such an extension of the classification is attempted in appendix V. Further, a suggestion for a classification of accounting in communist countries (as in the 1980s) is shown in appendix VI.

THE HYPOTHESIS

The classification shown in figure 6.1 was an hypothesis, in the sense that it was a testable suggestion about how various elements in a system fit together. The hypothesis may be tested in several ways. Chapters 6 and 7 deal with this testing.

The hypothesis in figure 6.1 borrows terminology from biology. Thus, Australian accounting is shown by the 'species' it belongs to, to be closer to UK accounting than it is to Netherlands accounting or to Canadian accounting. However, all these are closer to each other than to French accounting, which is in a different 'class' entirely. UK and Irish accounting are so similar that these individual systems could be said to be twins. There has also been borrowing from previous accounting classifiers. Thus some of Mueller's useful terminology has been adapted.

An attempt has been made to preserve hierarchical integrity. That

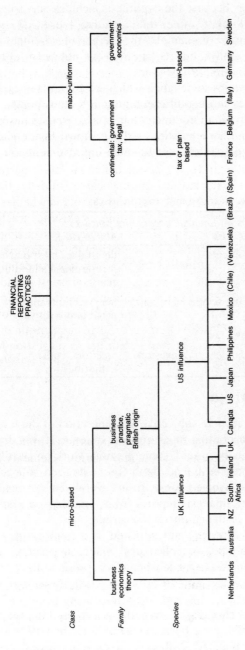

Figure 6.1 A suggested classification of accounting systems by practices

Notes:
1 Adjacency is not necessarily supposed to imply similarity. For example, it is not intended to imply that Australia is nearer to the Netherlands than the UK is.
2 The size of differences within a family varies from family to family.
3 Brackets indicate that a system may exhibit differences from others of its family because of lack of development.
4 See figure 8.1 for a final version.

is, each country is at the 'individual' level and belongs to a 'species', 'family', etc. However, because the hypothesis includes only some of those countries that *do* exist, rather than including those that *could*, some labels are missing. For example, the Netherlands belongs to a labelled 'class' and 'family', but its 'species' has not been labelled because there is no division at this point.

. Thus, figure 6.1 contains some labels which are attempts to explain the structural variables causing differentiation at various points. For example, the broad division into 'micro' and 'macro' classes has been performed using such characteristics as those shown in the simple morphology of table 6.1. In chapter 9, some improvements on this are suggested.

Table 6.1 Characteristics of micro and macro classes

| Factor | Effects on financial accounting practices | |
	Micro class	Macro class
1 Tax	small effects	determines most detailed measurement and valuation rules
2 Conservatism	prudence tempered by 'fair' view	heavy conservatism in profit and asset values
3 Objective	true and fair	correct and lawful
4 Users	shareholders and investors	creditors, bankers, tax authorities

PRELIMINARY TESTING

The hypothesis arose from a 'subjective' consideration of the factors which differentiate accounting measurement systems. It was drawn up in mid-1979. As has been said, some previous work on classification was included consciously; no doubt more entered subconsciously. The judgement involved comes from several years of reading books about, studying financial reports from, teaching on and (in some cases) teaching *in* the countries concerned.

The hypothesis was 'tested' and adjusted in a number of ways after mid-1979. A number of colleagues[1] made suggestions, and several useful comments were made when it was presented as part of various papers on five occasions.[2] Its broad structure always met with general agreement.

A second method of checking the hypothesis is to use the results of other researchers, which have been published since mid-1979 when the hypothesis was formulated. Although the present writer does not regard the groups generated by working on the Price Waterhouse data as superior to a 'subjectively' generated hypothesis (for the many reasons explained in chapters 3 and 5), it is interesting to compare the results. It becomes particularly clear that judgement is sooner or later necessary in order to use the work of the researchers discussed in the previous chapter because they come to different conclusions. At this point the process becomes rather circular: a set of results in search of a theory. In this case, the 'measurement' classification by Nair and Frank will be used (see p. 53). However, will this act as useful support for the hypothesis, or will the fact that their results best fit the hypothesis be a method of supporting their results against the others?

Taking Nair and Frank's 1973 or 1975/6 groupings, as far as they relate to the countries included in figure 6.1, produces the groups in table 6.2. This fits well with the hypothesis. The 'class' distinction takes groups I and IV together and groups II and III together. There is some slight difficulty over the Netherlands, Spain and Italy.

Table 6.2 Nair and Frank's groups for countries in figure 6.1

I	II	III	IV
Australia	Argentina	Belgium	Canada
Netherlands	Brazil	France	Japan
New Zealand	Italy (1975/6)	Germany	Mexico
Ireland	Spain (1975/6)	Italy (1973)	US
South Africa		Spain (1973)	
UK		Sweden	

As for the Netherlands, some of the difficulty is no doubt accounted for by the great diversity of practice there. Perhaps 'subjective' assessments stress too much the minority practices relating to re-placement cost accounting, but perhaps the Price Waterhouse data do not pick up the underlying differences in structure that might make the Netherlands react differently to the UK group: for example, the influence of the theory of microeconomics in the Netherlands.

Italy and Spain share many of the features of the other countries in group III, particularly France. Their accounting systems are, how-ever, rather less developed than those in France or Germany. Perhaps later data will reveal a catching up. It is certainly not a surprise that Spain exhibits some of the features of South American accounting.

The case of Japan is a difficult one because of the nature of its accounting development, although the hypothesis and the groups do fit here.

Japanese 'medieval' bookkeeping is overlaid with German practice introduced at the end of the nineteenth century, followed by a substantial influx of US practices after World War II (Nobes and Maeda 1990). Nair and Frank's 'disclosure' classifications place Japan with Germany rather than the US for 1973 (431), but with Germany *and* the US in 1975/6 (436).

FACTOR ANALYSIS

Despite the doubts registered at length about the use of data such as that provided by the Price Waterhouse survey (see pp. 55–60), it was decided to carry out tests on it. This was done partly because of the specific doubts about the results of Da Costa, Bourgeois and Lawson (see p. 49). Also, there was the important difference that an hypothesis had now been formed. Having completed and presented the first results in early 1980, there was sufficient encouragement to continue. These results are presented below. They help to divide the universe into two parts – 'micro' and 'macro' classes.

The first attempt to use the Price Waterhouse data of 1973 and 1975/6 to split countries into two groups was presented in early 1980 and published later that year.[3] The initial analysis for principal components found that the first seven components explained only 52 per cent and 42 per cent of the variance respectively (see table 6.3). This differs from the Da Costa, Bourgeois and Lawson (DBL) research where 60 per cent of the variance was explained by their first seven factors. The present research needed up to twelve factors to explain this much. Both seven and twelve factors were tried.

Table 6.3 Principal component analyses

	Cumulative percentage variance explained							
(a) *1973 survey*								
No. of factors	1	2	3	4	5	6	7	12
% variance	18	27	34	41	45	49	52	67
(b) *1975/6 survey*								
No. of factors	1	2	3	4	5	6	7	12
% variance	18	25	31	35	39	43	47	61

Further, the method of scoring each country on each factor used by DBL was simply to sum the scores for each attribute which showed a significant (greater than 0.4) correlation for that factor. Although this method may well make clustering easier (implicitly scores on attributes are given weight 0 or 1, and hence fewer attributes enter into

Table 6.4 Q-analyses

		Cumulative percentage variance explained		
(a)	*1973 survey*			
		No. of factors		
		1	2	3
A	Significant scores (7 factors)	63	83	90
B	Significant scores (12 factors)	61	82	89
C	P component scores (7 factors)	37	56	70
D	P component scores (12 factors)	27	42	53
(b)	*1975/6 survey*			
		No. of factors		
		1	2	3
A	Significant scores (7 factors)	71	86	94
B	Significant scores (12 factors)	69	83	92
C	P component scores (7 factors)	38	57	72
D	P component scores (12 factors)	29	44	56

the calculation), information about the original data may well be lost in the process. Thus, the alternative of using the actual principal component scores was also used as an input to the Q-analysis. This second part of the process was described in chapter 5, and consists of calculating the correlations of each country with each factor.

Figure 6.4 shows the degree of variance explained by different number of factors. It also shows the variance explained by the four successive Q-analyses. The simplifying nature of using just the significant scores for the Q-analysis becomes very clear. Table 6.5 shows, however, that broadly similar results may be obtained, even though the factor loadings differ in size, when correlations with the first factor are tried.

An examination of the 1973 and 1975/6 loadings on factor one produce the groups in table 6.6 for the countries in the hypothesis of figure 6.1. There seems to be strong backing for that hypothesis here. Column 1 represents the 'micro' class, and columns II and III the 'macro' class. There is even backing for more detail than this: Germany and Sweden are not part of the 'French' or 'South American' families. Japan's accounting is, of course, the problem; but its curious Germanic-American development seems to fit with this. Nair and Frank (1980) usefully show that the somewhat ambivalent scores of Germany, Sweden and Japan may be much connected with mixing disclosure and measurement practices. For all that, an initial broad brush bifurcation seems to have been very successfully established.

Table 6.5 Correlations with first factor from 'Q-analysis'

Country	A	B	C	D	Significant factors
Argentina	.74 (.73)	.70 (.66)	.49 (.44)	.47 (.31)	1,3
Australia	−.75 (−.88)	−.73 (−.86)	−.66 (−.68)	−.45 (−.59)	1,2
Bahamas	−.95 (−.94)	−.94 (−.93)	−.65 (−.55)	−.55 (−.46)	1
Belgium	.83 (.93)	.83 (.93)	.64 (.76)	.65 (.72)	1
Bermuda	(−.94)	(−.93)	(−.76)	(−.57)	1
Bolivia	.82 (.95)	.78 (.95)	.59 (.86)	.47 (.82)	1
Brazil	.89 (.97)	.90 (.98)	.79 (.82)	.70 (.80)	1
Canada	−.89 (−.93)	−.88 (−.93)	−.65 (−.73)	−.62 (−.62)	1
Chile	.79 (.94)	.75 (.93)	.50 (.52)	.41 (.38)	1
Colombia	.97 (.99)	.97 (.99)	.81 (.81)	.72 (.70)	1
Denmark	(.30)	(.35)	(.03)	(.00)	2,3
Ethiopia	.38 (.56)	.29 (.55)	.20 (.33)	−.05 (.23)	1,2
Fiji	−.62 (−.78)	−.57 (−.72)	−.55 (−.56)	−.33 (−.46)	1,2
France	.89 (.71)	.86 (.72)	.65 (.11)	.49 (.16)	1,3
Germany	−.28 (.12)	−.29 (.10)	−.21 (.12)	−.21 (.08)	2,3
Greece	(.97)	(.97)	(.63)	(.52)	1
India	.05 (.67)	.02 (.87)	−.04 (.24)	−.05 (.21)	1
Iran	(−.55)	(−.58)	(.10)	(.13)	1
Italy	.92 (.98)	.91 (.97)	.64 (.77)	.53 (.58)	1
Jamaica	−.86 (−.95)	−.86 (−.93)	−.72 (−.89)	−.65 (−.70)	1
Japan	.27 (−.21)	.25 (−.24)	.08 (−.09)	−.00 (−.05)	2
Kenya	−.97 (−.68)	−.96 (−.67)	−.96 (−.34)	−.75 (−.27)	1,2
Malaysia	(−.98)	(−.98)	(−.77)	(−.71)	1
Mexico	−.64 (−.87)	−.64 (.87)	−.32 (−.60)	−.29 (−.54)	1,2
Netherlands	−.91 (−.99)	−.91 (−.95)	−.42 (−.80)	−.40 (−.36)	1
New Zealand	−.72 (−.86)	−.69 (−.80)	−.65 (−.67)	−.44 (−.56)	1,2
Nigeria	(−.83)	(−.82)	(−.47)	(−.46)	1,2
Norway	(.83)	(.83)	(.40)	(.26)	1,3
Pakistan	−.25 (.65)	−.28 (.60)	−.28 (.22)	−.20 (.14)	1,3
Panama	88 (.87)	.79 (.82)	.63 (.49)	.35 (.42)	1,3
Paraguay	.97 (.98)	.97 (.98)	.91 (.88)	.79 (.86)	1
Peru	.79 (.61)	.73 (.54)	.58 (.40)	.44 (.38)	1,3
Philippines	−.75 (−.85)	−.76 (−.84)	−.40 (−.53)	−.43 (−.46)	1,2
Republic of Ireland	−.97 (−.97)	−.96 (−.97)	−.75 (−.86)	−.68 (−.79)	1
Rhodesia	−.91 (−.98)	−.84 (−.97)	−.87 (−.93)	−.68 (−.86)	1
Singapore	−.87 (−.94)	−.86 (−.92)	−.69 (−.83)	−.62 (−.75)	1
South Africa	−.96 (−.99)	−.94 (−.99)	−.89 (−.81)	−.75 (−.78)	1
Spain	.90 (.96)	.90 (.96)	.68 (.77)	.69 (.76)	1
Sweden	.34 (.27)	.35 (.32)	.17 (.04)	.17 (.06)	3
Switzerland	.83 (.89)	.80 (.90)	.29 (.53)	.27 (.43)	1
Trinidad and Tobago	−.66 (−.43)	−.60 (−.43)	−.67 (−.19)	−.43 (−.11)	1,2
United Kingdom	−.98 (−.99)	−.97 (−.99)	−.63 (−.91)	−.62 (−.85)	1
United States	−.83 (−.88)	−.83 (−.88)	−.38 (−.54)	−.44 (−.50)	1,2
Uruguay	.83 (.92)	.88 (.92)	.48 (.62)	.50 (.60)	1
Venezuela	.95 (−.77)	.95 (−.77)	.89 (−.20)	.86 (−.20)	1,2
Zaire	(.97)	(.96)	(.82)	(.80)	1

Notes: Figures in brackets are correlations for 1975/6 data.
  Column headings A to D relate to figure 6.5.

Table 6.6 Groups from table 6.5

Column I Strong negative correlations (>0.6)	Column II Less significant correlations	Column III Strong positive correlations (>0.6)
* Australia	Ethiopia	* Argentina
Bahamas	* Germany	* Belgium
* Canada	India	Bolivia
Fiji	(1973 only)	* Brazil
Jamaica	* Japan	Chile
Kenya	Pakistan	Colombia
* Mexico	(1973 only)	* France
* Netherlands	* Sweden	India (1975/6 only)
* New Zealand	Trinidad	* Italy
Philippines	(1975/6 only)	Pakistan
* Republic of Ireland		(1975/6 only)
Rhodesia		Panama
(Zimbabwe)		Paraguay
Singapore		Peru
* South Africa		* Spain
Trinidad		Switzerland
(1973 only)		Uruguay
* UK		Venezuela
* USA		(1973 only)
Venezuela		
(1975/6 only)		

Notes: The correlations are drawn from column A of table 6.5, and relate to those
    countries included in both 1973 and 1975/6 surveys.
    * = included in the hypothesis in figure 6.1.

ALTERNATIVE ATTEMPTS TO CLUSTER

Other methods are available to produce clusters from a mass of data
such as the Price Waterhouse surveys. Some of these methods are
described further in chapter 7. The methods of 'clustering by furthest
neighbour' and 'clustering by K-means' were used for all three
surveys. As examples, table 6.7 shows the results for the 1976 survey
and for a three-group clustering using 'K-means'; and table 6.8
shows a six-group clustering using 'furthest neighbour'. Both of
these fit remarkably well with the hypothetical classification in
figure 6.1.

The conclusions to be drawn from the work described in this
chapter are discussed in chapter 8. Before that, chapter 7
reviews testing which was not based on the Price Waterhouse
data.

Table 6.7 Clustering using 'K-means': 1976 survey

Cluster 1	Belgium
	Brazil
	France
	Italy
	Spain
Cluster 2	Australia
	Canada
	Mexico
	Netherlands
	New Zealand
	Republic of Ireland
	South Africa
	UK
	USA
Cluster 3	Argentina
	Germany
	Japan
	Sweden

Table 6.8 Clustering using 'furthest neighbour': 1973 survey

Cluster 1	Argentina
Cluster 2	Australia
	New Zealand
	South Africa
	Sweden
Cluster 3	Netherlands
	Republic of Ireland
	UK
Cluster 4	Belgium
	Brazil
	France
	Italy
	Spain
Cluster 5	Canada
	Mexico
	USA
Cluster 6	Germany
	Japan

NOTES

1 I am particularly grateful to Professor R. H. Parker for comments on the first draft.
2 AUTA conference, Loughborough, April 1980; Monash University, July 1980; University of Tasmania, July 1980; University of New South Wales, August 1980; Australian National University, August 1980.
3 Presented at AUTA conference, Loughborough, April 1980; published in *AUTA Review*, Autumn 1980.

7 A morphology and its use

In this chapter a new start is made on examining the proposed classification in figure 6.1. The previous chapter looked at tests of the classification using Price Waterhouse data; this chapter does not use that data but begins by construction of a 'subjective' morphology. This is then 'scored'. The results are used to see whether the 'prediction' of figure 6.1 can be confirmed.

CONSTRUCTION OF A MORPHOLOGY: SELECTING THE FACTORS

The task here is to identify the important differentiating factors in accounting measurement systems. A preliminary decision has to be made about whether to include economic, environmental and developmental factors in order to avoid the 'man as a featherless biped' or the 'Israel with Mexico' problems of chapter 3. It has been decided, however, to omit many such factors directly on the grounds that they do not constitute accounting practice and that they beg questions about which are the important developmental influences.

For example, the inclusion of 'language' as a factor seems too far removed from accounting to be usefully discriminatory. It is perhaps better to use this as a test of whether such factors can explain differences in accounting practice, as Frank (1979: 600–4) and Nair and Frank (1980: 437–44) do. Further, to include political systems or economic systems may be too vague. The fact that Western developed countries (the great bulk of which are democracies with mixed economies) are the main concern of the hypothesis in figure 6.1 already exhausts most of the differentiating power of such factors.

The reverse problem is that it may be important to avoid excessive detail in order consequently to avoid transitory and superficial differences. The fact that the UK moved in the 1970s from fully deferring tax (under SSAP 11) to partially deferring tax (under SSAP 15) may not constitute an important change of system or structure, though it obviously affected profit figures greatly. On the other hand, when taken together with other differences of this nature between US and UK accounting, perhaps a 'species' differentiation can be made, as in table 7.1. The common thread here appears to be the greater strictness of the US accounting practice; it is more tied to historical cost accounting and prudence. However, as has been mentioned, the differences are precarious: SSAP 11 which was in force at one time in the 1970s was very similar to APB 11; ED 14 on R&D was very similar to FAS 2; a US standard (FAS 52) was issued in 1981 to replace FAS 8. The new standard requires the use of the closing rate method. Such differences as this remain in the 1990s, although many of them are different from those of 1980 (Nobes 1988; Coopers and Lybrand Deloitte 1990).

Table 7.1 Some differences in accounting standards between the USA and the UK, 1980

	USA	*UK*
Deferred tax	APB 11 Full allocation	SSAP 15 Partial deferral
Research and development	FAS 2 Immediate expensing	SSAP 14 Some carry forward of development
Currency translation	FAS 8 Temporal method	ED 27 Closing rate method (in practice)
Fixed asset revaluation	Generally not allowed	Few restrictions

Thus, steering between the Scylla of vague, irrelevant factors and the Charybdis of transitory detail, the factors in table 7.2 were alighted upon. These are not justified on an 'empirical' basis; as pointed out several times in earlier chapters, it would be impossible to justify them by recourse to the Price Waterhouse data because that would merely assume that selection of practices (chosen for another purpose) was a better selection than one's own. The difference here, however, from such classifications as those by Hatfield, Mueller, Seidler and others mentioned in chapter 4 is that the selection of factors – the morphology – has been made more explicit. This has several advantages. First, others can inspect it, improve it,

Table 7.2 Factors for differentiation

Factor no. (and abbreviation	Factor name
1 (USER)	Type of users of the published accounts of the listed companies
2 (LAW)	Degree to which law or standards prescribe in detail, and exclude judgement
3 (TAX)	Importance of tax rules in measurement
4 (PRU)	Conservatism/prudence (e.g. valuation of buildings, stocks, debtors)
5 (HC)	Strictness of application of historical cost (in the historical cost accounts)
6 (RC)	Susceptibility to replacement cost adjustments in main or supplementary accounts
7 (CONS)	Consolidation
8 (PROV)	Ability to be generous with provisions (as opposed to reserves) and to smooth income
9 (UNI)	Uniformity between companies in application of rules

agree with it and so on. Second, it can be used to add further countries or to repeat the procedure in a later year.

However, the factors in table 7.2 have been chosen specifically in order to differentiate between the countries involved (see below). An extension of this to include various South American countries might have to include a factor about general purchasing power accounting. Although it is clear that this would differentiate between many South American countries and the rest of the world, it would have to be decided whether this factor really presented an important structural difference in accounting systems.

One problem with the factors in table 7.2 is that some of them still seem to be 'explanatory' rather than 'measurement' practices. It is not straightforward to separate them. However, it is clear that at least the first two factors are examples of the former. Other factors are less clear. For example, the 'taxation' factor could be taken as a factor explaining differences or, by scoring this factor on the basis of whether particular valuations are affected by tax rules, it could be seen as a measurement practice. All the factors except the first two have been taken in this latter sense, and scored using examples of practice.

This difficulty is shared by all the studies mentioned in the first section of this paper, where a number of characteristics like 'conservatism' or 'tax effects' were included. In this case, two separate exercises are carried out. First, factors 1, 2 and 3 are analysed as explanatory variables; then, factors 3 to 9 are analysed as measurement practices.

Before this can be done, the nine factors must be measured for each of the countries to be included. For the purpose of this testing, fourteen countries were chosen. All are developed Western nations, all were in the original 1979 hypothesis in figure 6.1 and are all included in all three of the Price Waterhouse surveys. Further, all the countries considered to be 'vital' by Mason (1978: ch. 6) for the purposes of international harmonization are included. These countries are France, Japan, Netherlands, UK, USA and Germany.

Table 7.3 Morphology based on table 7.2

Factor	0	1	2	3
1 (USER)	banks, revenue		institutions	individuals
2 (LAW)	detailed prescription			lack of prescriptions, much room for judgement
3 (TAX)	nearly all figs determined			no figures determined
4 (PRU)	heavy conservatism			dominance of accruals
5 (HC)	no exceptions			many exceptions
6 (RC)	no susceptibility	small experimentation	supplementary	used, considered for all
7 (CONS)	rare consolidation	some consolidation	domestic subsids	all subsids + assocs
8 (PROV)	considerable flexibility			no room for smoothing
9 (UNI)	compulsory accounting plan			no standardized format, rules or definitions

Scoring each country on the factors

The information for the scoring of each country was undertaken from works of reference, study of financial reports and (for each country except Japan and Sweden) either a period of working in the country concerned or detailed questionnaires on the country's accounting practices. The basis of scoring is described in 'morphology' form in table 7.3; the scores are set out in table 7.4. Again, in contrast to the earlier 'subjective' studies, these matters are made explicit and open

Table 7.4 Scoring based on table 7.3

	Australia	Belgium	Canada	France	Germany	Italy	Japan	Netherlands	New Zealand	R. of Ireland	Spain	Sweden	UK	USA
1 (USER)	3	1	3	1	0	1	0	2	3	2	1	0	2	3
2 (LAW)	3	1	2	1	0	1	1	3	3	2	1	1	2	1
3 (TAX)	3	0	3	0	0	1	0	3	3	3	1	0	3	2
4 (PRU)	2	0	2	0	0	0	0	3	2	2	0	0	2	2
5 (HC)	2	1	1	1	0	0	0	3	2	3	1	0	3	1
6 (RC)	2	1	2	1	0	0	0	3	2	2	0	1	2	2
7 (CONS)	3	1	3	1	2	0	1	3	3	3	0	2	3	3
8 (PROV)	2	1	2	1	1	1	0	2	2	2	1	0	2	3
9 (UNI)	3	0	3	0	1	2	1	3	3	3	0	1	3	3

to inspection. Appendix VII provides justifications for the scores in each case. The caveats relating to Italy and Sweden, mentioned at the beginning of chapter 6, should be remembered.

The scale 0 to 3 in table 7.3 was chosen on the grounds that it compromised between a smaller scale, which would have restricted differentiation, and a larger scale, which would have exaggerated the fineness with which judgement is possible. It is clear that one problem is the implied assumption of linearity. However, it is also a problem with all the previous research, and the results in the following figures may be seen to be so clear that some other reasonable assumption would not alter the classification seriously.

It may also be noted that the 'direction' of the factors could be altered, that is, that factor 4 could have had 'heavy conservatism' with a score of '3' (see table 7.3). This is dealt with by concentrating on differences or roots of squared differences, as seen below.

A further matter to consider is what weights the factors should have. The implication in all the previous research reviewed and reported here is that all practices have equal weight. This procedure is continued here, but the analysis is repeated with three of the factors being given double weight to see if the results are sensitive to such adjustments.

Finally, one might be criticized for adding different factors to-gether as though they were measured in the same units. This is connected with the weighting problem. All previous researchers had to do this addition, which perhaps may not be so serious when dealing with the *differences* on scores, and in the light of the clear results which follow.

ANALYSIS

The final stage is to analyse these figures in order to produce a classification. Several methods are attempted.

1 Totalling

A simple analysis is merely to total the scores. This assumes linearity in the scoring system, and assumes that none of the factors is 'back to front'. However, the extremely clean split of the countries into two groups (as in table 7.5) may reduce concern about these problems. Table 7.5 presents a straightforward division of the countries included into two groups. The high-scoring countries correspond with the 'micro' group of figure 6.1, and the low scoring countries with the 'macro' group. The exception is Japan, which will be discussed later. This split is clear both for the explanatory variables and for the measurement practices. Having established that the two point in the same direction, the rest of the analysis will proceed with measurement practices only, as it is these which are to be classified.

Table 7.5 Totals from table 7.4

	Practices	Explanatory
Netherlands	20	8
United Kingdom	18	7
Ireland	18	7
Australia	17	9
New Zealand	17	9
Canada	16	8
United States	16	6
France	4	2
Italy	4	3
Belgium	4	2
Sweden	4	1
Germany	4	0
Spain	3	3
Japan	2	1

2 Totalling differences

A somewhat more sophisticated approach is to calculate the sum of the differences on the factors, taking all possible pairs of countries. For example, using the scored morphology of table 7.4, one might find the difference in the scores of Australia and Belgium on factor 1

Table 7.6 Matrix of total differences between countries

	Aus	Bel	Can	Fra	Ger	Ita	Jap	NL	NZ	Ire	Spa	Swe	UK	USA
Australia	0													
Belgium	13	0												
Canada	1	12	0											
France	13	0	12	0										
Germany	13	4	12	4	0									
Italy	13	6	12	6	4	0								
Japan	15	4	14	4	2	4	0							
Netherlands	3	16	4	16	16	16	18	0						
New Zealand	0	13	1	13	13	13	15	3	0					
Ireland	1	14	2	14	14	14	16	2	1	0				
Spain	14	3	13	3	5	3	5	17	14	15	0			
Sweden	13	4	12	4	2	6	2	16	13	14	7	0		
United Kingdom	1	14	2	14	14	14	16	2	1	0	15	14	0	
United States	3	12	2	12	12	12	14	6	3	4	13	12	4	0

and add this to the difference on factor 2, and so on. This would give a matrix of differences as shown in table 7.6. The difference in scores for the pair Australia–Belgium is seen to be '13'. The information may be rearranged to focus on one country at a time by listing out the differences between it and each other country. This is shown in table 7.7.

Table 7.7 Like and unlike countries

	Like		*Unlike*	
AUSTRALIA	Australia	(0)	Belgium	(13)
(or New Zealand)	Canada	(1)	France	(13)
	Netherlands	(3)	Germany	(13)
	New Zealand	(0)	Italy	(13)
	Ireland	(1)	Japan	(15)
	UK	(1)	Spain	(14)
	USA	(3)	Sweden	(13)
BELGIUM	Belgium	(0)	Australia	(13)
(or France)	France	(0)	Canada	(12)
	Germany	(4)	Netherlands	(16)
	Italy	(6)	New Zealand	(13)
	Japan	(4)	Ireland	(14)
	Spain	(3)	UK	(14)
	Sweden	(4)	USA	(12)
CANADA	Australia	(1)	Belgium	(12)
	Canada	(0)	France	(12)
	Netherlands	(4)	Germany	(12)
	New Zealand	(1)	Italy	(12)
	Ireland	(2)	Japan	(14)
	UK	(2)	Spain	(13)
	USA	(2)	Sweden	(12)

Table 7.7 (cont'd)

	Like		Unlike	
GERMANY	Belgium	(4)	Australia	(13)
	France	(4)	Canada	(12)
	Germany	(0)	Netherlands	(16)
	Italy	(4)	New Zealand	(13)
	Japan	(2)	Ireland	(14)
	Spain	(5)	UK	(14)
	Sweden	(2)	USA	(12)
ITALY	Belgium	(6)	Australia	(13)
	France	(6)	Canada	(12)
	Germany	(4)	Netherlands	(16)
	Italy	(0)	New Zealand	(13)
	Japan	(4)	Ireland	(14)
	Spain	(3)	UK	(14)
	Sweden	(6)	USA	(12)
JAPAN	Belgium	(4)	Australia	(15)
	France	(4)	Canada	(14)
	Germany	(2)	Netherlands	(18)
	Italy	(4)	New Zealand	(15)
	Japan	(0)	Ireland	(16)
	Spain	(5)	UK	(16)
	Sweden	(2)	USA	(14)
NETHERLANDS	Australia	(3)	Belgium	(16)
	Canada	(4)	France	(16)
	Netherlands	(0)	Germany	(16)
	New Zealand	(3)	Italy	(16)
	Ireland	(2)	Japan	(18)
	UK	(2)	Spain	(17)
	USA	(6)	Sweden	(16)
REPUBLIC OF IRELAND (or UK)	Australia	(1)	Belgium	(14)
	Canada	(2)	France	(14)
	Netherlands	(2)	Germany	(14)
	New Zealand	(1)	Italy	(14)
	Ireland	(0)	Japan	(16)
	UK	(0)	Spain	(15)
	USA	(4)	Sweden	(14)
SPAIN	Belgium	(3)	Australia	(14)
	France	(3)	Canada	(13)
	Germany	(5)	Netherlands	(17)
	Italy	(3)	New Zealand	(14)
	Japan	(5)	Ireland	(15)
	Spain	(0)	UK	(15)
	Sweden	(7)	USA	(13)

Table 7.7 (cont'd)

	Like		Unlike	
SWEDEN	Belgium	(4)	Australia	(13)
	France	(4)	Canada	(12)
	Germany	(2)	Netherlands	(16)
	Italy	(6)	New Zealand	(13)
	Japan	(2)	Ireland	(14)
	Spain	(7)	UK	(14)
	Sweden	(0)	USA	(12)
USA	Australia	(3)	Belgium	(12)
	Canada	(2)	France	(12)
	Netherlands	(6)	Germany	(12)
	New Zealand	(3)	Italy	(12)
	Ireland	(4)	Japan	(14)
	UK	(4)	Spain	(13)
	USA	(0)	Sweden	(12)

Note: The numbers in brackets are the differences between the country concerned and the country to the left. The numbers come from table 7.6.

This technique may be preferable to the simple totals of table 7.5. First, it avoids the need to ensure that all the factors have been placed in the correct 'direction', that is that a country with a high score on one factor will tend to score highly on another. When concentrating on differences, it would not matter if, say, factor 4 had scored 'heavy conservatism' as '3' and 'dominance of accruals' as '0'. Second, concentrating on differences reveals that countries with similar total scores in table 7.5 may nevertheless be significantly different from each other. For example, Italy and France have identical total scores in table 7.5, but these totals have somewhat different causes. Thus, Italy and France are differentiated in table 7.6 or table 7.7.

Table 7.8 Groups of countries from table 7.7

Micro	Netherlands UK, Ireland, Australia, New Zealand, Canada USA
Macro	France, Belgium, Spain Italy Germany, Japan, Sweden

By inspection of the information in tables 7.6 and 7.7, groupings as in table 7.8 may be prepared. Again, apart from Japan, the simple classification which results seems to fit with figure 6.1.

3 Squaring the differences

The production of the squares of differences and the roots of squares of differences leads to analogous results to those in table 7.6, and thus the remarks in previous sections apply. The roots of the squared differences are used for clustering as described below. They may be inspected in appendix VIII.

4 Clustering by nearest neighbours

The next approach is to use this output (the roots of the squared differences) in a systematic way to produce clusters. A computer program designed to do this was used.[1] This starts with the two countries which are nearest to each other (in this case, Belgium and France, which have identical scores, see appendix VIII). Next it identifies another set of two or more similar countries. That is, in this case, Australia and New Zealand, which are closer together than Belgium plus France plus x (see p. 134). Thus, there are now twelve clusters: Australia plus New Zealand, Belgium plus France and ten clusters of one country each. This process continues, culminating in a 'two-cluster solution' (p. 139), which has the same groups as table 7.5 and 7.8 and (apart from Japan) figure 6.1.

Interesting information may be obtained by noting which countries are classified last. Italy is the last to fall into the 'macro' group. This seems very reasonable. Italy has seen dramatic changes in accounting in the last few years (see ch. 2 and appendix II); most of these have been excluded from the 1980 scoring process, but the fact that they have occurred suggests that the country must have been different from its 'macro' neighbours *before* they occurred. The USA is the last to be included in the 'micro' group; this seems reasonable for a group which starts off clustering around Australia and New Zealand.

5 Clustering by furthest neighbours

A very similar technique to that immediately above is to cluster by dissimilarity rather than similarity.[1] This merely attempts the clustering process in the reverse order to that above (for extracts, see appendix VIII). The two-group clustering gives an identical answer to tables 7.5 and 7.8. However, the four-group cluster is somewhat different from that obtained by 'nearest neighbour'-clustering. The 'furthest neighbour' four-group cluster is shown in table 7.9.

Table 7.9 Four-group clustering by 'furthest neighbour'

1	2	3	4
Australia	Netherlands	Belgium	Germany
Canada	Ireland	France	Japan
New Zealand	UK	Italy	Sweden
USA		Spain	

This seems plausible, but it illustrates one of the problems of clustering. The data used here for clustering do not suggest that Australia is more like the USA than the UK, as table 7.7 shows. However, table 7.9 does suggest this. The confusion arises because the USA is the last 'micro' country to fall into a group, and it is easier for the program to get the USA into group 1 of table 7.9 than to get the whole of group 2 into group 1 instead. The 'problem' arises because Australia plus New Zealand and UK plus Ireland set themselves up as groups in the early stages of clustering. Once the clusters have thus been 'seeded', they tend to grow and to resist combination with other clusters. If the clustering process were seeded around the USA and the UK, slightly different groups would emerge. Indeed, a group consisting of Australia, New Zealand, Ireland and the UK has a considerably smaller 'total internal difference'[2] than the group of Australia, Canada, New Zealand and the USA. However, the groupings are very stable, even if factors 3, 4 and 5 are given double weighting or if Australia, Ireland and Belgium (which have identical scores to New Zealand, the UK and France, respectively, and thus seed immediate clusters) are omitted.

NOTES

1 See K. V. Mardia, *et al.* (1979).
2 'Total internal difference' merely sums the differences on each pair of countries, using the differences in tables 7.6 and 7.7. For Australia, New Zealand, Ireland and the UK, the total internal difference is 4; for the alternative group, as in table 7.9, the difference is 10.

8 Comments on 1980 work

SYNTHESIS

There are many reasons for interest in the size and nature of the differences between financial reporting practices in different countries. These include the rise of multinational companies and accounting firms, an increased awareness of the value of examining the accounting problems and solutions of other countries and the continuing programme of international and EC harmonization.

As with many subject areas, initial activity is particularly concerned with a *description* of differences. If this is done accurately and in detail, it is a worthy and, indeed, essential activity. Later work seeks to understand the causes of the differences and to classify the individual elements into groups. This book begins by discussing the likely causes of international differences in financial reporting and then discusses a few important differences which seem to follow from these.

As an example, one might contrast financial reporting in France and the UK. In the former country, there is a codified legal system, comparatively few listed companies, centralized economic government, and prevalent bank and family interests in companies. Thus, it is possible to understand why published financial reporting and auditing, which are particularly associated with private shareholders, developed later and are less important than in the UK. One may also understand that the requirements of government lead to enhanced importance of taxation and of uniformity of measurement and presentation. This also leads to a greater requirement for objectivity, which may render unattractive the subjective Anglo-Saxon practices of allowing 'fairness' to override and of experimentation with replacement cost accounting. Further, in France, since banks, governments and taxation authorities may find consolidation irrelevant or contrary to their purposes, and since there is a comparative scarcity of private shareholders who might benefit from consolidation, the under-developed state of French consolidation was explicable. Finally, the youth, the smallness and the absence of an important role for the private professional accounting bodies in France may be explained by the early dominance of the government in rule-making and by the comparative unimportance of auditing. In turn, the lack of power reduces the profession's ability to experiment, to develop new practice and to make rules in new areas like consolidation.

Having studied such influences and important differences it may be possible to describe the essence of the financial reporting in a country using relatively few factors. It might then be possible to proceed to classification, which seems to be a fundamental part of much scientific study. Before attempting this in international accounting, it is sensible to try to learn from classifiers in other disciplines.

Examination of classification in other physical and social sciences suggests that the most useful parallel for our purposes is biological classification. Other physical sciences deal with elements which are too immutable and objectively measureable to be comparable. In chemistry, for example, the 'natural' classification by atomic number eventually became obvious and uncontroversial. In other social sciences, classifications so far have been rudimentary. However, biologists use a very sophisticated and detailed classification system which has a lengthy history. They have to use judgement in selecting the factors with which to classify and the locations at which to draw boundaries between groups. Further, they have to cope with a dynamic population which may render some boundaries quite arbitrary and ephemeral. One important point which emerges from the study of biological classification is that, for that field at least, a large input of judgement is an essential part of a scientific classification.

In comparative accounting, classification has been attempted several times. The purposes of such classification are several; and many of them apply in analogous ways to other subject areas. For a scientist or academic, classification is an obvious tool for better description, analysis and grouping of data. Discernment of a hitherto hidden order enables inferences to be made about the properties, backgrounds and relationships of elements in a system. Classification may also be of practical use for accountants connected with multinational companies as they prepare financial statements, consolidate them, audit them, assess comparative performance, move from one country to another, and so on. Classification may short-circuit the process of learning about and dealing with international variations in practices by clarifying important differences and similarities. Furthermore, given that harmonization has now much force behind it, classification may be important as an indicator of difficulties and of progress in harmonization.

The earliest classifications in comparative accounting were, not surprisingly, lacking in sophistication. Several attempts were made in the 1960s and 1970s, using background knowledge and judgement. In an effort to make classification less subjective and more scientific, attention in the late 1970s began to be directed towards large databases of accounting characteristics, like those by the AICPA (1964, 1975) and Price Waterhouse (1973, 1976, 1979). However, concern may reasonably be expressed at the use of a database designed for another purpose, especially one which may also be faulted more directly. Further, the *generation* of a classification by statistical methods seems unsound scientifically. Biologists are much more careful in the selection of appropriate data, and more ready to input substantial amounts of judgement.

CONCLUSIONS ON AN ACCOUNTING CLASSIFICATION

This section reports on several different attempts to improve upon previous classifications by stricter definition of the universe, the early formulation of an hypothetical classification containing more detail than hitherto, the open choice of factors on which to classify and the judgemental scoring of countries on factors. This allows more detail and more inspection than the early classifications, and involves more relevant data and more judgement than the later classifications.

In figure 6.1, the initial hypothetical classification with a hierarchy was set out. Inspection by specialist academics and comparison with some previous 'empirical' classifications suggested that it might be sufficiently plausible to justify testing it in more detail.

Price Waterhouse data from three surveys was used to test the hypothetical classification. The methods of previous researchers were approximately duplicated, and reasonable support for at least the initial split into two groups was obtained (see table 6.6). Furthermore, Germany and Sweden were identified as those countries which fitted least well with other continental European countries. This also supports the hypothesis in figure 6.1. The only difficulty arose with Japan, whose similarity with Germany was suggested by these results.

Further analysis of the Price Waterhouse surveys was undertaken using computer programs specifically designed to produce clusters. The results of different methods and different years were somewhat contradictory. In particular, the 1980 survey led to results at variance with the earlier surveys and with figure 6.1. This may be because of the very large number of 'not applicable' scores in that survey. Scoring these as either '0' or '6' may be misleading.

Despite these difficulties, it is easy to find support for figure 6.1. For example, the method of 'K-means' used on 1976 data (as in table 6.7) and the method of 'furthest neighbour' used on 1973 data (as in table 6.8) provide fairly startling support. By that stage it was fairly clear that the Price Waterhouse data might indeed be usable for classification, despite the criticisms of earlier chapters. There was also a clear suggestion that Japan should be seen with Germany, not with the USA.

Chapter 7 reported on a quite different approach to clustering. The eighteen countries of figure 6.1 were slightly reduced to the fourteen with which the author was able to become reasonably familiar. Then, after a programme of reading and visits, nine factors were chosen as important discriminating variables for accounting measurement and valuation practices. These nine were scored 'subjectively' but openly, and then several statistical techniques designed to produce groupings were carried out.

This work suggested strongly that the initial split into two classes of figure 6.1 was correct, except for Japan. Further splitting was also achieved, also along the lines originally predicted.

The conclusions of all this may be presented in a slightly revised version of the initial hypothetical classification. This is shown in figure 8.1, and may be regarded as the author's tested hypothesis. However, there are some difficulties with a straightforward classification of countries like Italy and Sweden. The largest of companies in these countries behave in an increasingly Anglo-Saxon way, due partly to specific rules applying to them only and partly to the need to raise funds in London or New York.

CLASSIFICATION AND HARMONIZATION

Having classified, it is natural to turn one's attention to harmonization. The thesis on which this work is based included a substantial section on harmonization which will be briefly summarized here before extending the discussion to the links between classification and harmonization. Harmonization is also discussed at greater length in Mason (1976) and Nobes (1990).

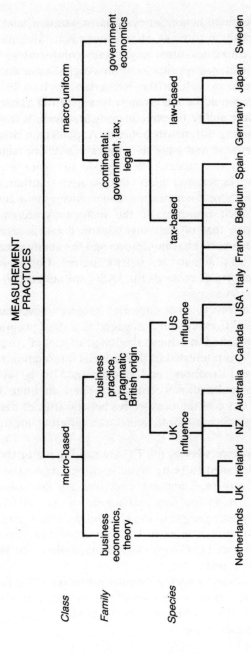

Figure 8.1 Tested hypothetical classification of measurement practices of listed companies in fourteen developed countries in 1980

Summary on harmonization

There are many potential beneficiaries of harmonization, and some of these are in a position to make efforts towards it. Multinational companies and accountancy firms might gain considerably. Their sphere of greatest influence appears to be the Anglo-Saxon world (as defined in this work to include the Netherlands). It is in these countries that there would be the greatest benefits from harmonization and the greatest ability to exercise pressure towards it. Also, many of the accounting differences between Anglo-Saxon countries are relatively superficial and easy to remove. Once one starts to include countries on the 'macro', 'legal' side of figure 8.1, the differences become larger and more deep-seated. Further, most accounting rules in those countries are under government control. The influence in such countries of the indigenous accountancy professions, let alone that of the Anglo-Saxon firms, is relatively slight. Thus the pressures for harmonization and the ability to carry it out through extra-legal activity are strictly limited. Consequently, such professional efforts as those of the IASC are unlikely to meet with substantial, direct success.

Harmonization involving such countries requires governmental interference. The EC Commission is engaged in a large programme of harmonization designed to achieve the long-run goal of creating a 'common market'. It is interested in the financial information reaching shareholders and creditors, and is concerned to be able to monitor and control multinational companies. These are quite different purposes from those of the prospective beneficiaries of harmonization in the Anglo-Saxon world, and quite different means are needed.

The company law directives of the EC are causing major changes in EC countries, designed to bring about harmonization. The difficulties of passing and implementing directives are not surprising when one bears in mind the size and nature of the differences. Furthermore, taking the example of the UK and the 1981 Companies Act, although substantial changes in UK accounting practices were required and can be traced to German legislation, much of the British accounting tradition remains.

Thus, both internationally and specifically within the EC, harmonization is turning out to be a very slow process which may never be fully completed. There are also severe doubts about its real desirability, as discussed below.

The links between classification and harmonization

A classification like that in figure 8.1 is heavily influenced, as is biological classification, by evolutionary considerations. A country's accounting practices are bound up with where they came from; and those countries whose accounting has similar origins usually have similar practices. Similarly, those countries with similar practices tend to have similar background factors like laws and ownership structures. Consequently, figure 8.1 is designed to represent a classification which is not based on superficial characteristics and is not ephemeral. This makes it clear that there are good reasons for international differences in accounting practices; different accounting is suited to different countries. In turn, this raises a fundamental question about the rationale for harmonization. Despite the advantages of harmonization to companies, accounting firms, governments and other users, these may be outweighed by the disadvantage of subverting various national accounting practices away from the optimal ones for domestic purposes. If some international differences are only accidental or superficial, as they may be between some Anglo-Saxon countries, perhaps their removal does no harm. However, many differences are more deep-seated and should perhaps be preserved.

Acknowledgement that this may be a serious problem leads to the proposal that harmonization should perhaps only apply to those companies with international dimensions. These are relatively few, and might be required to prepare accounts under both domestic and international rules.

A second connection between classification and harmonization is that the former may illustrate how difficult it will be to harmonize. Because of the long-run background differences, attempts to change accounting may have serious implications and may meet severe obstacles. Further, classification should show which countries might be the easiest to harmonize and which the most difficult.

For example, directing attention to figure 8.1, harmonization in the Anglo-Saxon world might seem a good place to start. The background and evolutionary factors are similar, and the profession has considerable power and much to gain from harmonization. Further, the commercial links between companies and firms from these countries are very great.

However, the most powerful force behind harmonization seems to be emanating from Brussels. Table 8.1, which contains the EC countries, suggests that the job of the EC Commission will be very difficult. Harmonization is proposed for countries on opposite sides of the classification in figure 8.1. Moreover, such harmonization would move the countries of the Anglo-Saxon world further apart. A classification, such as that in figure 8.1, is useful in that it reminds one of this latter problem of harmonization.

Table 8.1 Classification of EC countries

Micro 'fair'	Macro 'legal'
UK	France
Ireland	Germany
Netherlands	Belgium
Italy (? listed and state companies)	Luxembourg
Denmark	Italy
	Greece
	Spain
	Portugal

A further use of classification in the context of harmonization is that it may be a measure of the success of the latter. Figure 8.1 was drawn up in the context of the practices ruling in 1980, before the implementation of the Fourth Directive in the EC. If, after ten years, this and other harmonizing measures have been successful, one would expect to see shifts of countries when classifying using the various techniques discussed earlier.

Further research

Some ideas for further research spring naturally from the work reported on here. First, the preceding paragraph raises the prospect of a continuing programme of classifications, aimed at charting the progress of harmonization and other changes. This would involve a repetition of the scoring process in later years, preferably carried out by visits to, and detailed discussions with, accountants of the relevant countries. It may be necessary to update the factors used for classification, in a similar way to the occasional updating of the basket of goods used for the Retail Prices Index or the basket of shares used for the Financial Times Index. These indices are continuing series despite these changes of factors. An example in accounting is the price-change accounting issue; such a factor seems relevant now, but was only *potentially* relevant, for most countries in figure 8.1 for practical purposes, before the 1970s.

Second, it is clearly possible to extend the work to include other developed Western countries, most obviously those of South America. It would probably be necessary to add a factor related to a rapidly changing general price level. Such work would require more detailed study and data collection, as well as the input of judgement to amend the list of factors.

Third, one might consider extending or duplicating the classification to include matters other than measurement characteristics. A separate classification of disclosure would be possible. Also, one might consider management accounting or small company accounting or, even, bookkeeping systems. Classifications of these might be less interesting because the subjects may differ less internationally, or may be vaguer, or may have little importance for harmonization. Such a broadening might enable the more sensible inclusion of countries which have few or no large public companies who publish financial statements. As long as definitions and scope are made clear and used consistently for any classification, interesting and useful results may be obtainable.

A fourth line of further research would be to investigate further how classifications might be tailored to be most useful for particular persons or organizations. One might conduct research among multinational companies and accountancy firms to see what use could be made of classifications and which sorts were most useful.

9 Developments in the 1980s

This chapter brings this book up-to-date for the decade up to the end of 1990. The developments are discussed under four headings:

1 published research;
2 second thoughts on classification schemes;
3 changes in accounting practices leading to potential reclassifications; and
4 a classification of regulation in accounting.

PUBLISHED RESEARCH

Some papers after 1980 have been included in earlier chapters, for example those by Goodrich in chapter 5. Other papers have since been written within the same framework. Doupnik (1987) notes the criticisms of Nobes (1981) of the Price Waterhouse data. He asks a subset of seventy of the 1975 Price Waterhouse questions of managing partners of the original forty-six countries, and receives usable replies from thirty-six. He then repeats the classification methodology used by Nair and Frank (1980). He notes a decrease in differences over the period 1975 to 1983, and also some convergence of practice around IASC requirements.

Shoenthal (1989) purports to show that the competencies of newly qualified auditors in the UK and US could be used as one classifying variable. However, there must be doubt about whether this variable picks up anything relevant; and a two-country study can tell us nothing except that the two countries are different (Nobes 1991b; Shoenthal 1991).

Other publications (e.g. Choi and Mueller 1985; Berry 1987) have picked up the author's classification scheme, particularly from Nobes (1983). Also, the methodology of chapter 7 was applied by Al Najjar

(1986) to the classification of degrees of standardization, with an emphasis on four countries.

Using more judgemental methods, Puxty *et al.* (1987) classified accounting regulatory systems in four countries; and Gray (1988) examined cultural influences on the development of accounting in different countries.

SECOND THOUGHTS ON CLASSIFICATION SCHEMES

As a result of comments by others on the first classification, both published (Ryan 1985) and unpublished,[1] rethinking of the classification was possible. In particular, it now seems possible to refine the original classification (e.g. figure 8.1) in several ways, including the answering of four questions:

(a) What exactly is being classified?
(b) In what sense is the classification an hypothesis?
(c) Is the analogy with the Linnaean system reasonable?
(d) What is the meaning of the labelling on the classification?

These questions are addressed by Nobes and Roberts (1989). The last point will be discussed here.

The easiest solution to the problem of the exact meaning of labels is to omit them. But labels are inherent in any classification: otherwise what are the words 'birds' or 'lizards' in a Linnaean classification? Nevertheless, we should ensure that the labels capture the commonality implied by the attributes shared by the objects of the classifications. Also, we should make it clear that the words attached to a classification *are* to be understood merely as labels.

A further problem for classifications which are internationally oriented is cultural relativism. Attempts to use one set of cultural views to analyse another may lead to a breakdown of understanding. The relevance of this for figure 8.1 is that labels such as 'pragmatic' have a cultural loading. This may be inevitable, and a classification should come with a caveat that it might be misleading if read by those from cultures other than the classifier.

A second dimension of labelling in figure 8.1 is the use of Linnaean terminology to describe the various levels of the hierarchy ('species', 'families' and so on). Although it is clear that these labels are simply used as indicators of successive levels of generalization, one could question the suitability of using this terminology. For example, the term 'species' and its meaning have been subject to wide debate (Mayr 1976). In the post-Darwinian period, the term has a specifically

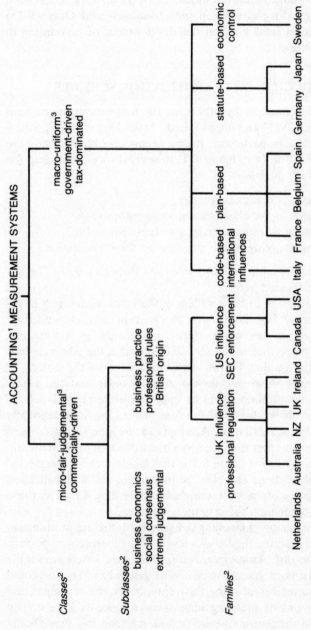

Figure 9.1 A suggested classification of accounting measurement 'systems' in some developed Western countries

Notes:
1. This is an abbreviated term for corporate financial reporting.
2. These terms, while borrowed from biology, should be interpreted merely as loose labels.
3. The terms at these and other branching points are merely labels to be used as short-hand to try to capture some of the attributes of the members of the accounting systems below them. This classification has been prepared by a UK researcher and may contain usage of terms that will mislead those from other cultures.

evolutionary connotation, which may not fit well throughout figure 8.1.

Again, one solution would be to remove the labels. However, labels can be useful short-hand: 'the USA and Canada are in the same family in figure 8.1'. Incidentally, it seems not to have been noticed by commentators that there are too many hierarchy labels in figure 8.1: two classes, four subclasses, four labelled families, fourteen individuals and an apparently spare label 'species'.

Bearing in mind all these observations, an improved version of figure 8.1 is suggested in figure 9.1, in which the following changes have been made:

(a) the title is changed to describe the suggested classification rather than the tests of it;
(b) the branching labels are changed to try to capture the most salient features of the groupings, and to remove the most culturally loaded labels (although some remain);
(c) Italy and Sweden move as a result of the greater clarity stemming from the new labelling;
(d) the term 'species' is removed as both superfluous and the most controversial of the hierarchical labels;
(e) some notes about interpretation are added

CHANGES IN ACCOUNTING PRACTICES

The changes

Since 1980, accounting has changed greatly in many countries. Some examples of changes are as follows.

The UK

The most obvious change is in the regulatory system. The Fourth and Seventh Directives of the EC were implemented by the 1981 and 1989 Companies Acts respectively. Although the measurement practices of accounting did not change greatly as a result, more uniformity was added to presentation.

In 1990, the professorial standard setting body was wound up in favour of a private body, the Accounting Standards Board.

As a result of inflation falling in the early 1980s, the experiments in current cost accounting were abandoned with great relief by companies and the profession.

Accounting standards had moved into more detailed areas, such as currency translation, lease accounting, merger accounting, pension accounting and segmental reporting.

The US

The regulatory system in the US remained much the same during the 1980s, although the Emerging Issues Taskforce was added to speed up the control of new and controversial areas.

In terms of practices, there was a move from the temporal method of currency translation to the closing rate method; and from the deferral method of deferred tax to the liability method.

Continental Europe

Great changes occurred in many continental countries. The Fourth Directive extended publication and audit to a large number of private companies. Disclosure increased dramatically in many countries. The Seventh Directive was coming into force from the late 1980s and leading to a dramatic extension of Anglo-American consolidation practices. The dates of implementation of these directives are shown in table 9.1, although the dates of bringing them into force are somewhat later.

Table 9.1 Implementation of directives

	Fourth	Seventh
Denmark	1981	1990
UK	1981	1989
France	1983	1985
Netherlands	1983	1988
Luxembourg	1984	1988
Belgium	1985	1990
W. Germany	1985	1985
Ireland	1986	–
Greece	1986	1987
Spain	1989	1989
Portugal	1989	–
Italy	1991	1991

Reclassification

These changes may be enough to alter the classification arrived at in chapter 8. This would involve the collection of data for the purposes of scoring countries to be included in the classification. The most recent large database (Gray *et al.* 1984) relates to practices of 1982, and therefore an exercise along the lines of those reported on in chapters 5 and 6 would presently not be possible. However, an exercise relying on smaller amounts of more relevant data (as in chapter 7) would be possible, and remains as a plausible research topic.

A CLASSIFICATION BY REGULATION

Most of this book has been concerned with the classification of countries by accounting practices or by underlying factors that might cause those practices. A further way of classifying countries is by the system of regulation used in accounting. (See table 9.2 for a list of abbreviations used in this section.)

Table 9.2 Abbreviations used in classification by regulation

Country	Abbreviation/acronym
Australia	AARF (Australian Accounting Research Foundation), ASC (Australian Securities Commission), ASRB (Accounting Standards Review Board), NCSC (National Companies and Securities Commission)
Canada	CICA (Canadian Institute of Chartered Accountants)
France	CNC (Conseil National de la Comptabilité), CNCC (Compagnie Nationale des Commissaires aux Comptes), COB (Commission des Opérations de Bourse)
Germany	WP Kammer (Wirtschaftsprüfer Kammer)
Japan	BADC (Business Accounting Deliberation Council)
Netherlands	CAR (Council for Annual Reporting), NIvRA (Nederlands Instituut van Registeraccountants)
UK	ASB (Accounting Standards Board), ASC (Accounting Standards Committee)
US	FASB (Financial Accounting Standards Board), SEC (Securities and Exchange Commission)

It is useful to separate the creation of rules from their enforcement. In the case of both activities, an obvious two-group classification of players is: government and non-government. Traditionally, in the English-speaking world (plus the Netherlands), the creation and enforcement of accounting rules has been in the hands of the profession. Initially the rules were not written down (e.g. in the UK up to the 1940s). Subsequently, they can be advisory for auditors (e.g. UK up to 1970 and Netherlands now); then compulsory for auditors because of professional rules (e.g. UK from 1970 and also some other major English-speaking countries now). Eventually, the rules (now generally called 'standards') may become compulsory even for companies (e.g. for US companies registered with the SEC; and in Canada and Australia because of insertion of standards into company law). In the UK, we have moved slightly towards this final position in that the Companies Act 1989 introduced the provision that directors of large companies must state whether they have complied with accounting standards.

The common feature about all the above positions is that standards are not set by the government. However, this bald statement is misleading in that the DTI in the UK, the SEC in the US and the ASRB in Australia stand closely by the rule makers. Clearly, the standard setters will make different rules if they know they can be enforced; hence the enormously more detailed and strict rules in the US compared to the UK.

A further subtlety is that these Anglo-Saxon non-governmental rule makers are not necessarily now the accountancy profession. In Canada and New Zealand they still are, but in the US this ceased to be the case with the formation of the FASB in 1972; and in the UK with the ASB in 1990. In Australia, a governmental standard-setting body (ASRB) was merged with the professional equivalent (the Accounting Standards Board of the AARF) in 1988, effectively leaving the profession in control because it appoints four of the nine members of the ASRB and it provides technical and administrative support. In the Netherlands, the standard-setting body (CAR) is a joint body of the profession (NIvRA) and the national organizations of employers and employees.

A second source of government influence is through company law statutes or commercial codes. These are central in the case of Germany and Japan, where no room has been left for the profession to command any significant part of rule making. In France there are statutes but most of the detail can be found in an accounting plan (*plan comptable général*) which is enforced by statute but controlled by a government committee (CNC). In Japan, the Ministry of Finance has the BADC which develops more detail than that contained in the law.

Another source of government influence is regulatory bodies to control securities markets and listed companies. The world's most obvious example is drawn from an Anglo-Saxon country; that is, the

SEC in the US, but there are weaker versions in the case of Australia (NCSC, ASC) and France (COB).

A complication for this analysis is that, just as the Anglo-Saxon non-governmental bodies are influenced by government, so the CNC (France), BADC (Japan) and the COB (France) are influenced from outside because they have many members from the business and accounting community.

Whereas Anglo-Saxon rule enforcement is achieved through a mixture of professional and governmental means, in continental Europe, enforcement, like creation, is largely governmental. The accounting rules can be enforced by statute; tax auditors help to impose accounting rules; and the auditing profession is controlled by bodies reporting to government ministries (e.g. the CNCC in France and the WP Kammer in Germany).

For the nine countries mentioned here, a classification of accounting rule making could be represented as in figure 9.2. Of course, the table loses a lot of detail, some of this can be captured in table 9.3, which scores the different rule makers in each country. The basic scores are for importance as a rule creator, with supplementary scores in brackets for rule enforcement. Let us examine the UK and Australia where there has been much recent change.

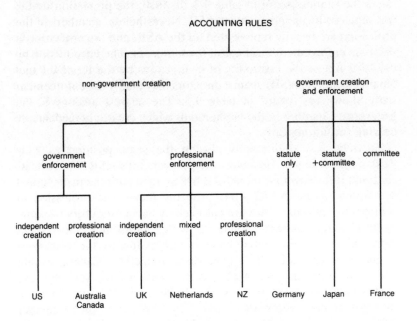

Figure 9.2 Classification of countries by rule making

Table 9.3 Creators and enforcers of financial reporting rules

	Statute law/code	Government comm./plan	SEC	Tax law	Court	Independent body	Profession
US	1	0	1(+2)	1	0	3	1(+1)
UK	2	0	0	0	0(+1)	3	1(+1)
CAN	1(+2)	0	0	0	0	0	3
AUS	1(+2)	1	0(+1)	0	0	0	3
NZ	1	0	0	0	0	0	3
NL	2	0	0	0	0(+1)	2	2
JAP	3	2	0	3	0	0	1
FRA	1	3	0(+1)	2	0	0	0
GER	3	0	0	3	0	0	0

Note: 0 = unimportant; 3 = very important.
Scores without brackets are for creators of rules; scores in brackets are extra scores for enforcement.

In the UK, the position until 1981 was as for New Zealand in table 9.3; that is (a) company law with few accounting rules except disclosure requirements, plus (b) more detailed accounting standards. The 1981 and 1989 British Companies Acts introduced a large number of accounting rules from directives of the EC, created by an institution with philosophical roots on the right of figure 9.2. This raises the 'statute' score in table 9.3. In 1990, the profession's ASC was replaced by an independent ASB. Nevertheless, members of the profession are heavily represented on the ASB, and the profession is the main enforcement mechanism for standards. The introduction by the 1989 Act of the possibility of civil actions by the Review Panel (connected to the ASB) against directors may justify the enforcement score shown for 'court' in table 9.3. The nearest analogy is the Enterprise Chamber in the Netherlands which creates precedents by hearing accounting cases.

Australia was traditionally also in the same position as New Zealand in table 9.3. However, the government's ASRB and NCSC confused this. Now that the ASRB has merged with the professional committee of the AARF, this probably leaves the profession in control of standards, which are enforced by having statutory backing. 'Statute' is thus shown in table 9.3 with a bracketed enforcement score, added to the initial creation score due to the disclosure requirements of schedule 7. (The same applies for Canada, where CICA is clearly in control of standard setting.) In Australia, the continued involvement of the ASRB, NCSC and ASC cause scores in the 'government committee' and 'SEC' columns. In September 1990, the AARF issued the Peirson Report which proposes the setting up of an independent Accounting Standards Board, which would be very similar to the new UK arrangements.

Despite the apparent chaos of the alphabet soup and the scores in table 9.3, the countries can at least be divided into two sorts as in figure 9.2. This will help in understanding how to operate and interpret accounting internationally.

NOTE

1 For example, by my colleague Alan Roberts and in a letter from Anthony Hopwood.

Appendices

These appendices support the original work on classification, as reported in various chapters of this book. Some suggestions for more up-to-date reading have been added in this edition.

Appendix I: Collection of data

The selection of factors by which to classify countries was carried out after an extensive programme of reading which was followed by visits to a great majority of the countries included. The list of references at the end of this appendix should be sufficient to back up the scoring in appendix VII.

The visits to the continental European countries listed below involved half-day discussions with English-speaking accountants working in firms affiliated to Anglo-American accountancy firms. Thus, these accountants were broadly familiar with differences between UK accounting and their own. It was upon the nature of the important differences that I concentrated.

Visits: (April and May 1981)

West Germany:	H. Holden, Arthur Young & Co, Frankfurt
Netherlands:	P. van der Zanden, Moret and Limperg, Eindhoven
France:	C. de Chastellux, Arthur Young & Co, Paris
Belgium:	A. Hardie, Arthur Young & Co, Brussels; and Mme Verdebout, ICHEC, Brussels
Italy:	M. Castelli, Arthur Young & Co, Rome; and A. Ruggeri, Deloitte Haskins & Sells, Florence
Spain:	R. Espinosa, Arthur Young & Co, Barcelona and J. Scannell, Coopers & Lybrand, Barcelona

Visiting posts

USA:	Fall Semester, 1978 – State University of New York at Albany, NY
Australia:	Term 2, 1980 – University of Tasmania, Hobart
New Zealand:	Term 2, 1981 – University of Auckland

Discussions in all these places used the questionnaire given at the end of appendix I as a starting point.

References for accounting in some countries considered in the text

France: Mueller (1967): 103–8
                  Beeny (1976)
                  Nobes and Parker (1981): ch. 4
                  Choi and Mueller (1978): chs 2 and 6
West Germany: Mueller (1967): ch. 4
                  Beeny (1975)
                  Macharzina (1981)
                  Choi and Mueller (1978): ch. 2 and 191–2
Netherlands: Mueller (1967): ch. 2
                  Muis (1975)
                  Klaassen (1980)
                  Nobes and Parker (1981): ch. 6
                  Choi and Mueller (1978): ch. 2 and 195–6
                  Beeny and Chastney (1978)
United States: Carsberg and Eastergard (1981)
                  Choi and Mueller (1978): ch. 2
                  Mueller (1967): ch. 3
                  Benston (1976)
                  Zeff (1972)
Canada: Carsberg and Eastergard (1981): 275, 281
                  Zeff (1972)
Sweden: Choi and Mueller (1978): 25, 38–40, 113, 114, 218,
                  219
                  Johansson (1965)
                  Mueller (1967): 27–30, 95–6, 108–9, 229
                  Price Waterhouse (1979) on consolidation and
                  equity method
Japan: Ohno *et al.* (1975)
                  Dale (1979)
                  Katsuyama (1976)
                  Ballon *et al.* (1975): chs 10 to 15
Italy: Stillwell (1976)
Belgium: Pauwels and Flower (forthcoming)
Spain: McRossin (1975)
                  Forrester (1981)
                  Donaghy and Laidler (1982)

More up-to-date references are:

> Nobes and Parker (1991a)
> Nobes (1988 and 1990)
> Coopers & Lybrand (1990)

YOUR HELP IS REQUESTED WITH THE FOLLOWING SURVEY:

I am trying to compile data on financial reporting practices in countries other than the UK and the USA; I would be very grateful if you could spare the time to fill in the following about your own country. I will let you know the results. Please leave this form with the conference secretariat. Thank you very much for your help.

> Chris Nobes,
> Economics Department
> Exeter University,
> Devon, UK

Questions for survey of published financial reporting of companies listed on a stock exchange.

1 Outline what you understand by a 'fair view' ....

2 Is such a 'fair view' the overriding goal, the main goal, or a subsidiary goal? ....

3 Where are the rules, if any, for what constitutes a 'fair view'? ....

4 Are the rules ever inconsistent with 'fairness' in individual cases?

5 Which figures in the financial statements might change if tax rules changed? In practice, are these figures different from what they would be if there were no tax rules on the particular subject?

6 To what extent are financial statements adjusted for price changes? ....

7 To what extent can any reserves or provisions or charges be altered in size in any particular year depending on how successful the year has been?..
....

8 Even in periods of unchanging prices, do your accounting practices lead to profit figures which could be said to be unrealistically low for the purpose of potential investors? For example, do financial analysts adjust profits upwards? ....
....

9 Is it very easy to identify the figure for profit after interest and tax but before extraordinary items? ....
....

10 Who do you consider to be the major users of published financial statements? ....
....

11 Does the law (company law or tax requirements) specify valuation requirements in some detail?...............................

NAME ....
UNIVERSITY ....

Appendix II: Accounting in Italy, Spain and Belgium

Italy

Although there are few who doubt the supremacy of Italian accounting in the thirteenth to fifteenth centuries, its state by the 1970s was regarded by many as lamentable. An ICAEW publication (Stillwell 1976) describes the situation as follows:

> There is no strong independent profession. Hampered by an exhaustive, Napoleonic-structured Civil Code and often used more as a device to thwart the tax authorities than to provide accurate results, the accounting of most Italian companies remains very much a family affair . . . tales of multiple sets of books, hidden records, and destroyed original records usually contain more truth than falsehood.
>
> In practice there is virtually no effective independent audit . . . Thus, what information is disclosed by Italian companies to their shareholders, to the tax authorities or to a potential foreign investor is largely at the discretion of the Italian management.

The types of company structure bear a strong similarity to those found in France, though there are far fewer listed companies. There is a commercial code, but no accounting plan. Traditionally tax rules have been the main means of control of accounting. This has meant that accounting figures are manoeuvred to reduce taxation, and that no 'provision for taxation' is shown as it might aid an inspector. The civil code does call for the disclosure of the true position but it was effectively overridden by the tax rules relating to the need to record in the books any accelerated depreciation, bad debt provisions or revaluations.

Depreciation may be claimed for tax purposes up to maximum rates allowed by the Ministry of Finance (e.g. buildings, 3–7 per cent

pa; plant and equipment, 10–25 per cent pa). Accelerated depreciation is available for the first three years of an asset's life, when an
extra 15 per cent is allowed. These amounts must be entered into the
financial accounts. For bad debt provisions the allowance is 0.5 per
cent per year until 2 per cent of debtors, followed by 0.2 per cent per
year until the total is 5 per cent of debtors. For stock valuation, LIFO
is generally used and encouraged by tax concessions. However, FIFO
and average cost are possible. Maintenance expenses cannot be
deducted without limit, but to a maximum of 5 per cent of written
down cost of the maintained asset – the rest to be written off equally
over the next five years. If this writing off is to be allowed, the
expenditure must be capitalized. Research and development may
only be written off by 50 per cent in the first year; then, if
unsuccessful, by 50 per cent in the following year or, if successful, by
equal installments over its period of providing benefit.

There were several important reforms which were initiated in the
mid-1970s and which have had substantial effects. One of these was
the reform of the personal and corporate taxation system on 1
January 1974. This reduced the arbitrariness of tax assessments by
limiting the power of inspectors. It has resulted in the partial freeing
of financial accounting from tax accounting. For example, it is now
practicable to take extra non-deductible provisions for bad debts, or
to have financial depreciation which does not agree with tax depreciation. However, it is still the case that tax relief will be delayed by not
accepting accelerated depreciation, and that there are tax disadvan-
tages to using the equity method, for example. Nevertheless, this
reform was significant in the context of the other reforms relating to
the introduction of new accounting principles for state and listed
companies, as mentioned in chapter 2. It allowed the room for the
new type of auditors to insist on a greater use of 'fairness' and the
accruals concept, despite the tax implications. The new auditors are
to carry out work in addition to the existing statutory audits by
sindaci, who will continue to sign that the statements are true (*veri*)
and real (*reale*).

One area where there has been little advance so far for listed
companies is consolidation. It has been difficult to persuade companies to involve themselves in the extra work necessary. However,
consolidation has been made compulsory for state companies and,
presumably, when CONSOB has firmly established the more basic
principles for listed companies, consolidation will be tackled. Also
there are no signs of replacement cost or other price adjusted
techniques of accounting.

It is also the case that the profit and loss account, while it is detailed, does not clearly present an 'earnings' figure but still uses a two-sided account. This and the lack of consolidation displays the continuing lack of orientation towards outside equity shareholders.

As for harmonization, in 1981 CONSOB called for the use of International Accounting Standards for listed companies. This follows the publication of new accounting principles, which are strongly linked to Anglo-American standards, by the committee of the *Ordine dei Dottore Commercialisti*. The more powerful instructions of the EEC Commission in the shape of company law directives relating to accounting have not yet been enacted in Italy.

General sources: Stillwell (1976) and discussions with Mauro Castelli of the Rome Office of Arthur Young & Co, and Andrea Ruggeri of the Florence Office of Deloitte Haskins & Sells.

Spain

Spanish corporate forms correspond well with those found elsewhere in continental Europe. Bank finance was particularly important in the 1940s and 1950s, until an encouragement of foreign investment began in 1959. SAs can be very small; shares are usually bearer; and there are no publication or filing requirements. Companies must obey the commercial code of 1885; the Act of 1951 demanding accounts which have *claridad y exactidad*; and a Royal decree of 5 September 1980 demanding prospectuses and regular publication of information in a *Boletin* for listed companies. The profession, too, resembles those of some parts of continental Europe in that it was formed recently (1943) and is fairly small (about 3,000). Members of the 'Institute of Sworn Account Censors' must be employed by a number of public authorities and by listed companies. Also, if 10 per cent of the shareholders of any public company are dissatisfied with their auditors, they may have a 'sworn censor' added to the committee. However, as in Italy, these audits are not onerous. It has been reported that the audit fee of one of the largest twenty Spanish companies was Ptas 100,000 (£750), whereas an Anglo-American firm quoted Ptas 3,000,000 (McRossin 1975).

Perhaps as few as 10 per cent of 'sworn censors' actually practice as auditors (Donaghy and Laidler 1982: 63). However, a reform of the 1951 Law was being considered during 1981 which would bring in a compulsory report by independent experts. It would also involve minimum capital requirements (5 m pesetas for SAs), two-tier boards and compulsory filing of accounts.

Thus, although the stock exchange requests that accounts should be 'reasonable' (*racionabilmente*), it is a weak body (about 700 shares are quoted). Also, there is no effective audit and the real rules come from taxation regulations. Even though companies are allowed to produce financial accounts which differ from the tax accounts, as in Italy before the late 1970s, there is an overriding tendency to keep them the same in order to avoid difficulties with tax inspectors.

Nevertheless it is not the case that all figures are determined by tax regulations. For depreciation, it is possible to choose within a range of figures, though where accelerated depreciation (e.g. 100 per cent regional allowances) are offered this will usually be accepted and 'booked'. Inventories are not determined by tax law and are not uniformly dealt with across companies. However, the methods chosen must be applied consistently. As from 1 January 1979, there are new corporation and income taxes. Some details will affect accounting. For example, formation expenses should now be written off over ten years, and a specific provision for bad debts may now be set up.

As for valuation of fixed assets, a fiscal revaluation as at 31 December 1978 and 31 December 1979 has been allowed using a government retail price index. This does affect depreciation unlike the French case. Thus there is a considerable incentive to revalue. Apart from this, there is no sign of price adjusted accounting yet, although indexed values should not be allowed to exceed current replacement cost.

As in Italian accounting, consolidation is rare and the earnings figure is unclear. In this case, the lack of clarity results partly from the treatment of tax as an appropriation. Bankers are important users of accounting information in Spain, and without a strong stock exchange or accounting profession, improvements for shareholders look less likely than in France or Italy.

Whereas the 'less developed' status of accounting in Italy is being gradually transformed, at least for state and listed companies, by reference to Anglo-Saxon accounting principles, the transformation in Spain is due to emulation of the French model. The most obvious manifestation of this is the progressive introduction of an accounting plan. The Ministry of Public Finance established the Institute of Accounting Planning in 1973 which has produced several versions of the plan for different sectors. There is a permanent controlling body called the *Consejo Nacional de Contabilidad*. As in France, the plan consists of a chart of accounts, a set of definitions, formats for annual accounts and valuation principles. The headings of the decimalized chart of accounts are in the same order as the French chart, though the sub-headings vary to some extent.

The plan began by being voluntary. By an Act of December 1973, the plan had to be used for those companies who wished to revalue. This continued for the 1978 and 1979 revaluations. However, by an Order of 14 January 1980, companies covered by plans already in issue must comply with those plans from 1981. The plans are being adjusted to make them consistent with the EC's Fourth Directive on company law, and international conferences have been held to harmonize the plans (e.g. in Paris in April 1980).

Thus, there is no similar sign to that in Italy that suggests a movement towards Anglo-Saxon accounting. Banks are still important users of accounts; the profession has little power or credibility; there are no accounting standards; the stock exchange or shareholder groups are not significant forces; and the government is intervening in favour of harmonization with French-type accounting.

General Sources: Forrester (1981) and Donaghy and Laidler (1982). Discussions with: R. Espinosa of the Barcelona Office of Arthur Young & Co, and J. Scannell of the Barcelona Office of Coopers & Lybrand.

Belgium

As might be expected, accounting in Belgium bears many similarities to accounting in France. In particular:

1 Financial accounts must be the same as tax accounts.
2 Consolidation accounting is rare. This is the case in Belgium even among listed companies. Also, the exact method of consolidation varies, and is not usually well explained. For example, the treatment of inter-company profits and stock holdings is unreliable.
3 There is a less strong use of materiality than in Anglo-Saxon countries.
4 An accounting plan (*Plan Comptable Minimum Normalisé*) is now compulsory. It is more restricted than the French, being mainly a chart. However, the other rules and definitions are contained in the laws of 1975 and 1976. The latter was responsible for introducing the plan. There had previously been a voluntary plan. This new Belgian plan had been designed to be consistent with the Fourth Directive, but a few changes will be necessary. The charts go to the Banque Nationale.

When tax requirements lead to a view which is not 'fair' (e.g. accelerated depreciation), the difference will be shown in an annex.

LIFO is allowed for inventory valuation.

Replacement cost value is allowed in published accounts, but there are no effects on profit because extra depreciation is added back. The practice is not common.

There is a lessening ability to operate income smoothing. Anglo-Saxon auditors and Belgian reviseurs are coming closer together on standards.

Users include suppliers and banks as well as analysts.

The 'earnings' figure is not directly stated, and there can be problems with provisions.

Source: Discussions with Mr A. Hardie of Arthur Young & Co, Brussels, and Mme Verebout of ICHEC, Brussels. For more up-to-date information on these three countries, see Nobes (1990).

Appendix III: Rules for the calculation of taxable income in the late 1970s in the UK, USA, France, West Germany and the Netherlands

As should be clear from chapter 2, the influence of taxation on accounting varies from negligible in the UK to dominant in France. Such is the importance of this difference for accounting that a simple classification of tax bases would look much like a simple classification of accounting systems. For example, a two-group classification in either case might put the UK, the USA and the Netherlands in one group, and France and Germany in the other.

In the former group the requirement for financial accounting to present a 'fair' view to shareholders pre-dates and overrides any taxation rules. Consequently many adjustments to accounting profit are necessary in order to arrive at the tax base: taxable profit. In the other group, the needs of taxation have been dominant in the evolution of accounting and auditing. Consequently, the tax base corresponds closely with accounting profit. It is a complaint of Anglo-Saxon accountants that the importance of this continental taxation effect is not even disclosed. However, as has been discussed, the EC's Fourth Directive should remedy this.

Tax bases have been discussed elsewhere, country by country (James and Nobes 1978: ch. 13; Chown 1974; Saunders 1977; Commerce Clearing House 1979). Here it is intended to discuss some of the differences between countries by topic.

Depreciation

Naturally, in all the countries studied in detail here, the revenue authorities take an interest in the amount of depreciation charged in the calculation of taxable income. This concern varies from fairly precise specification of rates and methods to be used (as in most countries), to an interference only where charges are unreasonable (as in the Netherlands). As has been pointed out in earlier chapters, the vital difference for *financial* accounting is that accounting depreciation must usually be kept the same as tax depreciation in Franco-German countries but not under Anglo-Saxon-Dutch accounting. An interesting effect of this difference is that there is little need for the concept of deferred taxation in Franco-German countries.

Examples of the specification of rates and methods for depreciation of fixed assets for tax purposes are shown below (European Taxation 1978; CCH 1979; James and Nobes 1978: ch. 12). They are up to date at least as far as 1978.

1 In the UK for 1980–81, machinery is depreciated 100 per cent in the first year; cars are depreciated at 25 per cent on a reducing balance basis. There is a complete separation of this scheme of 'capital allowances' from the depreciation charged by companies against accounting profit. Unlike other countries, the UK does not give any depreciation tax allowance for most commercial buildings.

2 In the US, for 1978, there were depreciation ranges for difference assets. For example, office furniture should be written off in eight to twelve years. This gives an implied straight-line rate. Alternatively, a reducing-balance rate of up to 150 per cent of the straight-line rate could be used. Other methods are acceptable. In addition, there was a 20 per cent initial bonus depreciation and a tax credit of 10 per cent of investment. There are other accelerated allowances from time to time.

3 In the Netherlands, since 1978, there has been a system of tax free investment premiums and bonuses. Depreciation may be determined by individual companies. Typical levels are: buildings 2 per cent, plant 10 per cent, cars 20 per cent. Straight-line depreciation may be used for any asset, and reducing balance for all assets except buildings. Companies may change from one method to another if there are good business reasons.

4 In France, depreciation is allowed by tax law on a straight-line basis for nearly all assets at the following rates: industrial and commercial buildings 5 per cent, office or residential buildings 4 per cent, plant and fixtures 10–20 per cent, vehicles 15–25 per cent. It is possible to use a reducing balance basis for plant. The rates to be used are expressed as multiples of the straight-line rates depending on the asset's life. It is possible to change the basis. Accelerated depreciation is allowed for R&D, certain regions, anti-pollution and energy saving assets.

5 In Germany, depreciation rates are specified by tax law. Straight-line is available for all assets, and mandatory for buildings, at the

following rates: buildings 2.5 per cent, plant 10 per cent, office equipment 20 per cent, office furniture 10 per cent, vehicles 20–25 per cent. It is possible to change methods only from reducing balance to straight-line. Accelerated allowances are available for assets in Berlin and Eastern border areas, and for anti-pollution.

Allowances for inflationary gains on inventories

The second largest adjustment made during the calculation of corporation tax liabilities in the UK since 1973 is 'stock relief' (James and Nobes 1978: ch. 12). This partially allows for the fact that, during periods of inflation, an important element of accounting and taxable profits is an unrealized gain due to holding trading stocks. This is not part of operating profit and there may be liquidity problems if it bears corporation tax. The relief in 1980 was equal to the difference between opening and closing stocks reduced by 15 per cent of taxable profit after capital allowances. Substantial changes were introduced in 1981.

In the US, the last-in-first-out (LIFO) system of inventory costing is allowed for both financial and tax accounting. During inflation this reduces stock valuation and increases the cost of sales expense, thus reducing accounting and taxable profits. In the other countries mentioned above, there is neither stock relief nor a deliberate use of LIFO to correct for holding gains. LIFO is allowed in Germany in those unusual cases where it corresponds with physical reality; in the Netherlands where it is commercially sensible; and in France never.

Capital gains

The taxation of corporate capital gains varies substantially by country. In the UK a proportion of capital gains is added to taxable income. In 1980–81, when corporation tax was 52 per cent, the proportion was 15/26; this means that the capital gain bears 30 per cent taxation, which is the same rate as the original individual capital gains tax.

In the Netherlands and Germany, capital gains are added to taxable income in full. In the US and France, short-term capital gains are fully taxed (US, under six months; France, under two years), but long-term capital gains are taxed at a reduced rate.

Losses

Different treatment of losses can have important effects on taxable profits. These are illustrated in table III.A.

Table III.A Operating loss reliefs (years)

	Carry back	Carry forward
UK	1	no limit
US	3	7
France	0	5
W Germany	1	5
Netherlands	1	6

Dividends received

The degree to which the dividends received by a company must be included has an important effect on its taxable income. In the UK, domestic dividends are not taxed in the hands of a recipient company. In the US, dividends from subsidiary companies are not taxed. However, 15 per cent of dividends from other companies in which there is at least a 10 per cent holding are taxed, and all dividends from companies held under 10 per cent are taxed. In France, dividend income is fully taxed unless there is a holding of at least 10 per cent or FF 10 m, in which case only 5 per cent of dividend income is taxed. In Germany, dividends are fully taxable unless they come from a company in which a 25 per cent or greater interest is held, in which case they are exempt. In the Netherlands, a minimum 5 per cent holding relieves dividends from tax.

Expenses

In the UK, the US and the Netherlands, a number of expenses deducted in the calculation of profit may not be allowed in the calculation of taxable income. In France and Germany, what is deducted for financial accounting generally depends on what is allowed for tax purposes. Most countries are more generous than the UK in allowing expenses for taxation. For example, most of them allow entertainment expenses to be deducted. In the three other European countries there are also greater allowances for bad debts and various other provisions.

Other taxes

A very important complicating factor in determining overall tax burdens is the existence, and degree of deductibility for national corporate income tax purposes, of other types of taxes on companies. In most countries there is some form of payroll tax or social security tax. In the UK there are local property 'rates'. In Germany there are regional income taxes, capital taxes and payroll taxes. In France there is a business licence tax. In Italy there is a regional corporation tax. In general these taxes are deductible in the calculation of national corporation tax. However, because of these taxes, the total tax burden is much higher than might be thought at first sight in countries like Germany where regional taxes are important.

For more up-to-date information, see James and Nobes (1988) and Nobes and Parker (1991, ch. 20).

Appendix IV: Classification of languages

The classification shown here in diagrammatic form is based on the description in chapter 4 of *Language* by Bloomfield (1935). It is not supposed to be exhaustive, and is more detailed in some parts than in others.

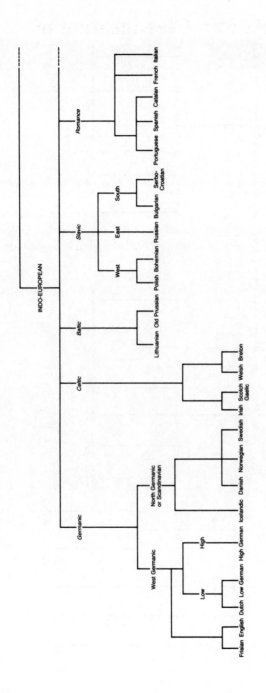

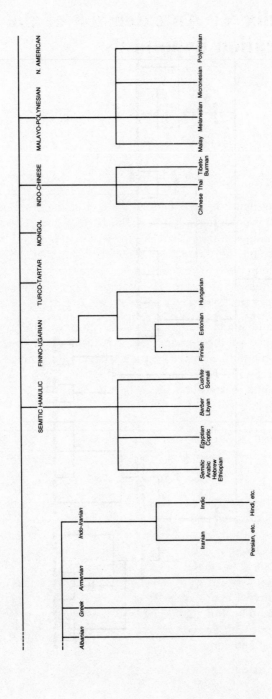

Appendix V: An extension of the classification hypothesis

The following figure is an expanded version of the corrected 1979 hypothesis. It is not intended to be seen as reliable but as summarizing various findings of the research of the writer and others. It tries to take into account, for example, the measurement classifications by Nair and Frank (1980). The countries included here are those in the Price Waterhouse surveys of 1973 and 1975/6, except for the following omissions:

1 Pakistan and India were omitted because of the contradictory evidence of the research about which group they belong to (see table 6.6). This is coupled with a reluctance to put them with South American or European systems because of developmental reasons and David and Brierley's second criterion (see ch. 3).
2 Ethiopia and Iran were omitted because of the uncertain nature of their political, social and economic conditions.
3 Greece was omitted because it was not in the 1973 survey and because it did not seem to fit with the group's tentatively suggested by the research.
4 Panama was omitted because of the conflicting results of the writer's research and that of Nair and Frank (for 1973).
5 Zaire was omitted because it was not in the 1973 survey and because, although it had been a Belgian colony, it seemed out of place with the continental European group.
6 Denmark and Norway were omitted because they did not appear in the 1973 survey, and because it is not clear in which part of the 'macro' group to put them. Table 6.5 would suggest that they should be put with Sweden, which seems eminently sensible on a geographical and cultural basis.

To a large extent, these omissions are due to lack of knowledge (which inspires caution) rather than to a weakness in the method of classification. With these nine omissions and the thirty-seven countries contained in the figure, the forty-six countries of the 1975/6 survey are accounted for.

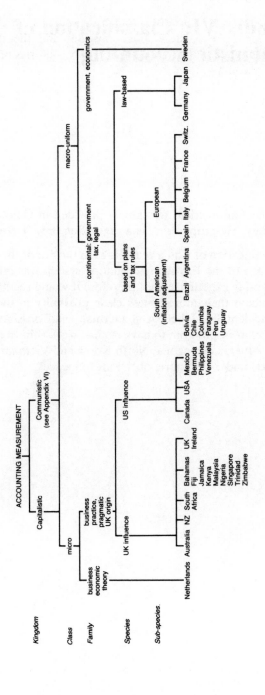

Appendix VI: Classification of communistic accounting

The classification overleaf was kindly provided in October 1980 by Derek Bailey. He proposed it as a suggestion only. He noted:

> The classification of China really is as in the era of the later Mao. The design of the Egyptian accounting system was influenced by the Yugoslav experience and, therefore it would seem reasonable to anticipate their more-or-less close proximity in the classification. Incidentally, I believe a German, and possibly a French influence, or inspiration, to have been at work. I have no information on Albania. Mongolia, North Korea and Vietnam would fall, I suspect, under the rubric of 'USSR influence'.

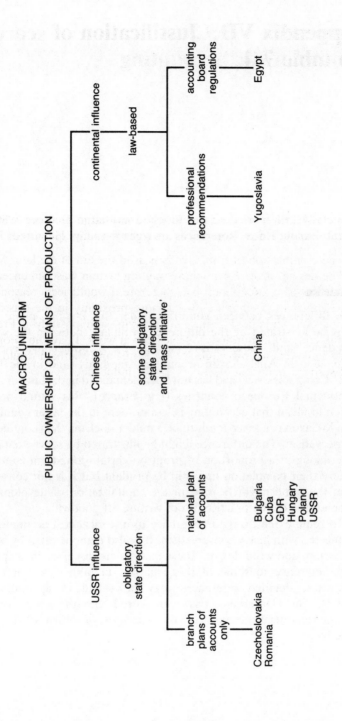

Appendix VII: Justification of scores in table 7.4

Generally, the scoring relates to listed and large companies in the countries concerned. References are to be found in appendices I and II.

Prudence

The differences between countries under this heading might perhaps be illustrated by the difference in nuance between the words 'prudence' and 'conservatism' (see ch. 2). Although 'prudence' is demanded in Anglo-Saxon accounting standards (and in the UK's 1981 Companies Act) and has not been demanded in the laws of some continental European countries (e.g. France), this should not be taken to mean that accounting is less prudent in the latter countries. Anglo-Saxon prudence tends to be a milder doctrine than continental conservatism. The difference might be illustrated by some examples. The taking of a proportion of profit on certain long-term contracts before their completion may still be prudent but it is not conservative; the same might be said of the capitalization of development expenditure or the practice of not writing off goodwill.

To some extent, a rigid adherence to historical cost accounting is connected with heavy conservatism. It is also demonstrated by lavish provisions and write-downs. These matters are discussed in chapter 2 with reference to some of the countries in table 7.4. For other countries, detailed references may be found in appendices I and II. The Netherlands has been scored with the lowest regard for conservatism because of the strength of 'fairness' in that country.

Historic cost

Those countries where the statutory accounts rigidly use historic cost (HC) have been scored as '0'. Scores of '3' mean that it is not only possible to revalue assets within the HC accounts, but also to substitute current cost as the main accounts. Scores of '2' recognize *ad hoc* revaluation. Spain, France and Belgium score '1' for 'organized' occasional revaluations.

Tax

Scores of '3' represent the determination of no figures in the financial statements by tax rules (apart, of course, from the 'tax' figures themselves). Scores of '0' represent dominance by tax rules for detailed valuation and measurement. A score of '2' for the USA records the fact that there is some interference with financial accounting because of the tax rules relating to investment credits and the use of LIFO. Scores of '1' represent the determination by tax rules of only some of the following: depreciation, bad debt provisions, stock values, revaluations, miscellaneous provisions.

Replacement cost

This factor relates to use of *supplementary* replacement cost (RC) or other current value data. Use in the main accounts is considered partly in factor 2. A score of '0' records no experimentation with supplementary RC information. A score of '3' represents well-established use of detailed supplementary statements (or main RC accounts). A score of '2' denotes significant, but recent, experimentation with RC accounting.

Users

Scores of '0' denote dominance by 'inside' users in the shape of governments, revenue authorities, bankers or families; Germany, Sweden and Japan seem to fit this. Other countries, like France, Italy or Spain have slightly more widespread ownership by private shareholders and efforts by stock exchange authorities to create 'fairer' accounting. Scores of '3' denote the largest emphasis on private, small shareholders. The UK, for example, only scores '2' because of the importance of institutional shareholdings and government finance.

Provisions

Japan and Sweden are famous for 'income smoothing', as the detailed references in appendix I will show; hence they score '0'. France and Germany score '1' for reasons illustrated in chapter 2. A score of '3' represents a strong stance against movements on reserves, against the creation of 'provisions for risks', and against arbitrary changes in values. The USA best typifies this.

Consolidation

It is necessary to remember that this scoring is designed to relate mainly to large and listed companies. Scores of '3' mean well-established consolidation of nearly all subsidiaries, and use of the equity method. Scores of '2' mean either lack of use of the equity method or lack of consolidation of foreign subsidiaries or lack of sufficient compulsion to ensure compliance. Scores of '1' mean recent or partially adopted consolidation practices. Scores of '0' mean that consolidation is rare, as in Italy and Spain.

Law

Countries which have very little company law or tax law on the subject of valuation or measurement, and where accounting standards are not detailed or not compulsory score '3'. The UK scores '2' because of a somewhat more extensive set of laws and standards than Australia or New Zealand, and because it has more powerful standards than the Netherlands. (After the 1981 Companies Act, a score of '1' might be more suitable.) The USA, despite little relevant company law, has very detailed standards which are government backed, and it has detailed mandatory disclosure requirements. Thus, it scores '1'.

Uniformity

This factor relates to the use of charts of accounts, the influence of which spills over into published accounts. These are compulsory in France, Belgium and Spain (hence a score of '0'). They are voluntary but influential in Germany and Sweden. In Italy, there is some standardization of formats and definitions. In the Anglo-Saxon world, in 1980, there were few examples of uniformity.

Appendix VIII: Computer output relating to chapter 7

Roots of squares of difference   p. 133
Clustering by nearest neighbours   pp. 134–9
Clustering by furthest neighbours   pp. 140–2

Distance Matrix (lower triangle)

		1	2	3	4	5	6	7	8	9	10
Australia	1	0.00									
Belgium	2	5.39	0.00								
Canada	3	1.00	5.29	0.00							
France	4	5.39	0.00	5.29	0.00						
Germany	5	5.20	2.00	4.90	2.00	0.00					
Italy	6	5.20	2.83	4.90	2.83	2.45	0.00				
Japan	7	5.74	2.00	5.48	2.00	1.41	2.00	0.00			
Netherlands	8	1.73	6.32	2.45	6.32	6.48	6.48	6.93	0.00		
New Zealand	9	0.00	5.39	1.00	5.39	5.20	5.20	5.74	1.73	0.00	
R. of Ireland	10	1.00	5.66	2.00	5.66	5.66	5.66	6.16	1.41	1.00	0.00
Spain	11	5.66	1.73	5.57	1.73	2.65	2.24	2.24	6.71	5.66	5.92
Sweden	12	5.20	2.00	4.90	2.00	1.41	2.83	1.41	6.32	5.20	5.66
UK	13	1.00	5.66	2.00	5.66	5.66	5.66	6.16	1.41	1.00	0.00
USA	14	1.73	5.10	1.41	5.10	4.69	4.90	5.48	2.83	1.73	2.45

		11	12	13	14
Spain	11	0.00			
Sweden	12	3.00	0.00		
UK	13	5.92	5.66	0.00	
USA	14	5.57	4.90	2.45	0.00

13 Cluster solution
Combining the cluster containing: 2 Belgium
  and the cluster containing: 4 France

1	Australia	1	1
2	Belgium	2	2
3	Canada	3	1
4	France	2	0
5	Germany	5	1
6	Italy	6	1
7	Japan	7	1
8	Netherlands	8	1
9	New Zealand	9	1
10	R. of Ireland	10	1
11	Spain	11	1
12	Sweden	12	1
13	UK	13	1
14	USA	14	1

12 Cluster solution
Combining the cluster containing: 1 Australia
  and the cluster containing: 9 New Zealand

1	Australia	1	2
2	Belgium	2	2
3	Canada	3	1
4	France	2	0
5	Germany	5	1
6	Italy	6	1
7	Japan	7	1
8	Netherlands	8	1
9	New Zealand	1	0
10	R. of Ireland	10	1
11	Spain	11	1
12	Sweden	12	1
13	UK	13	1
14	USA	14	1

11 Cluster solution
Combining the cluster containing: 10 R. of Ireland
and the cluster containing: 13 UK

1	Australia	1	2
2	Belgium	2	2
3	Canada	3	1
4	France	2	0
5	Germany	5	1
6	Italy	6	1
7	Japan	7	1
8	Netherlands	8	1
9	New Zealand	1	0
10	R. of Ireland	10	2
11	Spain	11	1
12	Sweden	12	1
13	UK	10	0
14	USA	14	1

10 Cluster solution
Combining the cluster containing: 1 Australia
and the cluster containing: 3 Canada

1	Australia	1	3
2	Belgium	2	2
3	Canada	1	0
4	France	2	0
5	Germany	5	1
6	Italy	6	1
7	Japan	7	1
8	Netherlands	8	1
9	New Zealand	1	0
10	R. of Ireland	10	2
11	Spain	11	1
12	Sweden	12	1
13	UK	10	0
14	USA	14	1

9 Cluster solution
Combining the cluster containing: 1 Australia
    and the cluster containing: 10 R. of Ireland

1	Australia	1	5
2	Belgium	2	2
3	Canada	1	0
4	France	2	0
5	Germany	5	1
6	Italy	6	1
7	Japan	7	1
8	Netherlands	8	1
9	New Zealand	1	0
10	R. of Ireland	1	0
11	Spain	11	1
12	Sweden	12	1
13	UK	1	0
14	USA	14	1

8 Cluster solution
Combining the cluster containing: 5 Germany
    and the cluster containing: 7 Japan

1	Australia	1	5
2	Belgium	2	2
3	Canada	1	0
4	France	2	0
5	Germany	5	2
6	Italy	6	1
7	Japan	5	0
8	Netherlands	8	1
9	New Zealand	1	0
10	R. of Ireland	1	0
11	Spain	11	1
12	Sweden	12	1
13	UK	1	0
14	USA	14	1

7 *Cluster solution*

Combining the cluster containing: 8 Netherlands
and the cluster containing: 10 R. of Ireland

1	Australia	1	6
2	Belgium	2	2
3	Canada	1	0
4	France	2	0
5	Germany	5	2
6	Italy	6	1
7	Japan	5	0
8	Netherlands	1	0
9	New Zealand	1	0
10	R. of Ireland	1	0
11	Spain	11	1
12	Sweden	12	1
13	UK	1	0
14	USA	14	1

6 *Cluster solution*

Combining the cluster containing: 5 Germany
and the cluster containing: 12 Sweden

1	Australia	1	6
2	Belgium	2	2
3	Canada	1	0
4	France	2	0
5	Germany	5	3
6	Italy	6	1
7	Japan	5	0
8	Netherlands	1	0
9	New Zealand	1	0
10	R. of Ireland	1	0
11	Spain	11	1
12	Sweden	5	0
13	UK	1	0
14	USA	14	1

5 Cluster solution

Combining the cluster containing: 3 Canada
               and the cluster containing: 14 USA

1	Australia	1	7
2	Belgium	2	2
3	Canada	1	0
4	France	2	0
5	Germany	5	3
6	Italy	6	1
7	Japan	5	0
8	Netherlands	1	0
9	New Zealand	1	0
10	R. of Ireland	1	0
11	Spain	11	1
12	Sweden	5	0
13	UK	1	0
14	USA	1	0

4 Cluster solution

Combining the cluster containing: 2 Belgium
               and the cluster containing: 11 Spain

1	Australia	1	7
2	Belgium	2	3
3	Canada	1	0
4	France	2	0
5	Germany	5	3
6	Italy	6	1
7	Japan	5	0
8	Netherlands	1	0
9	New Zealand	1	0
10	R. of Ireland	1	0
11	Spain	2	0
12	Sweden	5	0
13	UK	1	0
14	USA	1	0

3 Cluster solution

Combining the cluster containing: 2 Belgium
and the cluster containing: 5 Germany

1	Australia	1	7
2	Belgium	2	6
3	Canada	1	0
4	France	2	0
5	Germany	2	0
6	Italy	6	1
7	Japan	2	0
8	Netherlands	1	0
9	New Zealand	1	0
10	R. of Ireland	1	0
11	Spain	2	0
12	Sweden	2	0
13	UK	1	0
14	USA	1	0

2 Cluster solution

Combining the cluster containing: 6 Italy
and the cluster containing: 7 Japan

1	Australia	1	7
2	Belgium	2	7
3	Canada	1	0
4	France	2	0
5	Germany	2	0
6	Italy	2	0
7	Japan	2	0
8	Netherlands	1	0
9	New Zealand	1	0
10	R. of Ireland	1	0
11	Spain	2	0
12	Sweden	2	0
13	UK	1	0
14	USA	1	0

6 Cluster solution

Combining the cluster containing: 2 Belgium
and the cluster containing: 11 Spain

Cluster number	Observation number	Identification
1	1	Australia
	3	Canada
	9	New Zealand
2	2	Belgium
	4	France
	11	Spain
3	5	Germany
	7	Japan
	12	Sweden
4	6	Italy
5	8	Netherlands
	10	R. of Ireland
	13	UK
6	14	USA

5 Cluster solution

Combining the cluster containing: 1 Australia
and the cluster containing: 14 USA

Cluster number	Observation number	Identification
1	1	Australia
	3	Canada
	9	New Zealand
	14	USA
2	2	Belgium
	4	France
	11	Spain
3	5	Germany
	7	Japan
	12	Sweden
4	6	Italy
	8	Netherlands
	10	R. of Ireland
	13	UK

4 Cluster solution

Combining the cluster containing: 2 Belgium
and the cluster containing: 6 Italy

Cluster number	Observation number	Identification
1	1	Australia
	3	Canada
	9	New Zealand
	14	USA
2	2	Belgium
	4	France
	6	Italy
	11	Spain
3	5	Germany
	7	Japan
	12	Sweden
4	8	Netherlands
	10	R. of Ireland
	13	UK

3 Cluster solution

Combining the cluster containing: 1 Australia
and the cluster containing: 8 Netherlands

Cluster number	Observation number	Identification
1	1	Australia
	3	Canada
	8	Netherlands
	9	New Zealand
	10	R. of Ireland
	13	UK
	14	USA
2	2	Belgium
	4	France
	6	Italy
	11	Spain
3	5	Germany
	7	Japan
	12	Sweden

2 Cluster solution

Combining the cluster containing: 2 Belgium
and the cluster containing: 5 Germany

Cluster number	Observation number	Identification
1	1	Australia
	3	Canada
	8	Netherlands
	9	New Zealand
	10	R. of Ireland
	13	UK
	14	USA
2	2	Belgium
	4	France
	5	Germany
	6	Italy
	7	Japan
	11	Spain
	12	Sweden

Bibliography

Abel, R. (1969) 'A comparative simulation of German and US accounting principles', *Journal of Accounting Research*, Spring.

AICPA (1964) *Professional Accounting in 25 Countries*, New York.

AICPA (1975) *Professional Accounting in 30 Countries*, New York.

Al Najjar, F. (1986) 'Standardisation in accounting practices: a comparative international study', *International Journal of Accounting*, Spring.

American Accounting Association (AAA) (1977) *Accounting Review Supplement to Volume 52*.

Armstrong, J. S. (1967) 'Derivation of a theory by means of factor analysis', *American Statistician*, December.

Ballon, *et al.* (1975) *Financial Reporting in Japan*, New York: Kodansha Int. Ltd.

Beeny, J. H. (1975) *European Financial Reporting – 1*, London: ICAEW.

Beeny, J. H. (1976) *European Financial Reporting – 2*, London: ICAEW.

Beeny, J. H. and Chastney, J. C. (1978) *European Financial Reporting – 4*, London: ICAEW.

Benston, G. J. (1976) 'Public (US) compared to private (UK) regulation of corporate financial disclosure', *Accounting Review*, July.

Berry, A. (1987) 'The need to classify worldwide practices', *Accountancy*, October.

Bloomfield, L. (1935) *Language*, London: Allen and Unwin, chs 1 and 4.

Buckley, J. W. and M. H. (1974) *The Accounting Profession*, Los Angeles: Melville.

Carsberg, B. and Eastergard, A. (1981) 'Financial reporting in North America', in Nobes and Parker (1981).

CCH (Commerce Clearing House) (1979 and later editions) *United States Master Tax Guide*, Chicago: Commerce Clearing House.

Choi, F. D. S. and Mueller, G. G. (1978) *An Introduction to Multinational Accounting*, New Jersey: Prentice Hall.

Choi, F. D. S. and Mueller, G. G. (1985) *Frontiers of International Accounting*, UMI Research Press.

Chown, J. F. (1974) *Taxation and Multinational Enterprise*, Longman.

Coopers and Lybrand Deloitte (1990) *Accounting Comparisons: UK/US*.

Coxon, A. P. M. (1982) *Multidimensional Scaling*, London: Heinemann.

Da Costa, R. C., Bourgeois, J. C. and Lawson, W. M. (1978) 'A classification of international financial accounting practices', *International Journal of Accounting*, Spring.

Dale, B. (1979) 'Accounting in Japan', *Australian Accountant*, April.

David, R. and Brierley, J. E. C. (1978) *Major Legal Systems in the World Today*, London: Stevens.

Davidson, S. and Kohlmeier, J. (1966) 'A measure of the impact of some foreign accounting principles', *Journal of Accounting Research*, Autumn.

Donaghy, P. J. and Laidler, J. (1982) *European Financial Reporting –5*, London: ICAEW.

Doupnik, T. S. (1987) 'Evidence of international harmonisation of financial reporting', *International Journal of Accounting*, Fall.

Encyclopaedia Britannica, 'Classification, Biological', 15th edn, 4: 683–94.

European Taxation (1978) *Guides Volume II*, Amsterdam: International Bureau of Fiscal Documentation.

Flint, D. (1982) *A True and Fair View*, London: Gee.

Forrester, D. A. R. (ed.) (1981) *Spanish Accounting in the Past and Present*, University of Strathclyde: Strathclyde Convergencies, ch. 3.

Frank, W. G. (1979) 'An empirical analysis of international accounting principles', *Journal of Accounting Research*, Autumn.

Goodrich, P. S. (1982) 'A typology of international accounting principles and policies', *AUTA Review*, Spring.

Goodrich, P. S. (1983) 'A typology of international principles and policies: A reply to a comment', *AUTA Review*, Spring.

Gray, S. J. (1980) 'The impact of international accounting differences from a security-analysis perspective: some European evidence', *Journal of Accounting Research*, Spring.

Gray, S. J. (1988) 'Towards a theory of cultural influence on the development of accounting systems internationally', *Abacus*, March.

Gray, S. J., Campbell, L. G. and Shaw, J. C. (1984) *International Financial Reporting*, London: Macmillan.

Gregory, P. R. and Stuart, R. C. (1980) *Comparative Economic Systems*, Boston: Houghton Miflin, p. 21.

Hatfield, H. R. (1966) 'Some variations in accounting practices in England, France, Germany and the United States' *Journal of Accounting Research*, Autumn.

ICAEW (1980) *Survey of Published Accounts – 1908*, London: ICAEW, p. 40.

James, S. R. and Nobes, C. W. (1978) *The Economics of Taxation* (first edition), Philip Allan.

James, S. R. and Nobes, C.W. (1988) *The Economics of Taxation* (third edition), Philip Allan.

Johansson, S. (1965) 'An appraisal of the Swedish system of investment reserves', *International Journal of Accounting*, Fall.

Johnson, T. J. (1972) *Professions and Power*, London: Macmillan.

Kagan, K. K. (1955) *Three Great Systems of Jurisprudence*, London: Stevens.

Katsuyama (1976) 'Recent problems of the financial accounting system in Japan', *International Journal of Accounting*, Fall.

Kirkman, P. R. A. (1991) 'Accounting for price changes' in Nobes and Parker (1991).

Kitchen, J. (1972) 'The accounts of British holding company groups: development and attitudes to disclosure in the early years', *Accounting and Business Research*, Spring.

Klaassen, J. (1980) 'An accounting court: the impact of the Enterprise Chamber on financial reporting in the Netherlands', *Accounting Review*, April.

Lafferty, M. (1975) *Accounting in Europe*, Woodhead-Faulkner, Cambridge.

Macharzina, K. J. (1981) 'Financial reporting in West Germany', in Nobes and Parker (1981).

Mardia, K. V., Kent, J. T. and Bibby, J. M. (1979) *Multivariate Analysis*, London: Academic Press, pp. 369–75.

Mason, A. K. (1976) *International Financial Reporting Standards: Problems and Prospects*, ICRA Occasional Paper No. 13, Lancaster; also 'International reporting of inventories', *Accountant*, 7 October 1976.

Mason, A. K. (1978) *The Development of International Financial Reporting Standards*, ICRA Occasional Paper No. 17, Lancaster, pp. 21–2.

Mayr, E. (1976) 'Species, concepts and definitions' in M. Greve and E. Mendelsohn (eds), *Topics in the Philosophy of Biology*, Reidel.

McRossin, F. M. (1975) 'Spain – country at the crossroads', *Accountant's Magazine*, February.

Mueller, G. G. (1967) *International Accounting*, New York: Macmillan, Part 1.

Mueller, G. G. (1968) 'Accounting principles generally accepted in the United States versus those generally accepted elsewhere', *International Journal of Accounting*, Spring.

Muis, J. (1975) 'Current value accounting in the Netherlands: fact or fiction?', *Accountant's Magazine*, November.

Nair, R. D. and Frank, W. G. (1980) 'The impact of disclosure and measurement practices on international accounting classifications', *Accounting Review*, July.

Neuberger, E. and Duffy, W. (1976) *Comparative Economic Systems*, Boston: Allyn and Bason, chs. 6 to 9.

Nie *et al.* (1974) *Statistical Package for the Social Sciences*.

Nobes, C. W. (1981) 'An empirical analysis of international accounting principles – A comment', *Journal of Accounting Research*, Spring.

Nobes, C. W. (1982) 'A typology of international accounting principles and policies: A comment', *AUTA Review*, Spring.

Nobes, C. W. (1983) 'A reply to a reply', *AUTA Review*, Spring.

Nobes, C. W. (1988) *Interpreting US Financial Statements*, London: Butterworths.

Nobes, C. W. (1990) *Accounting Comparisons, UK/Europe*, Vols I, II and III, Cooper and Lybrand Europe.

Nobes, C. W. (1991a) 'Harmonisation of accounting', ch. 5 in Nobes and Parker (1991).

Nobes, C. W. (1991b) 'Classification by competencies: A comment', *Journal of Business Finance and Accounting*.

Nobes, C. W. and Maeda, S. (1990) 'Japanese accounts: an interpretation', *Accountancy*, September.

Nobes, C. W. and Matatko, J. (1980) 'Classification of national systems of accounting', *AUTA Review*, Autumn.

Nobes, C. W. and Parker, R. H. (1979) 'Landmarks in accounting history', *Accountancy*, June.

Nobes, C. W. and Parker, R. H. (1981) *Comparative International Accounting* (first edition), Philip Allan.

Nobes, C. W. and Parker, R. H. (1991) *Comparative International Accounting*, (third edition), Prentice Hall.

Nobes, C. W. and Roberts, A. D. (1989) 'Second thoughts on a judgemental international classification', University of Reading Discussion Papers.

Ohno, *et al.* (1975) 'Recent changes in accounting standards in Japan', *International Journal of Accounting*, Fall.

OECD (1980) *Accounting Practices in OECD Member Countries*, Paris: OECD.

Pauwels, P. A. and Flower, J. (forthcoming) *European Financial Reporting – 6*, London: ICAEW.

Previts, G. J. (1975) 'On the subject of methodology and models for international accountancy', *International Journal of Accounting*, Spring, 4.

Price Waterhouse (1973) *Accounting Principles and Reporting Practices: A Survey in 38 Countries*, London: ICAEW.

Price Waterhouse (1976) *Accounting Principles and Reporting Practices: A Survey in 46 Countries*, London: ICAEW.

Price Waterhouse (1979) *International Survey of Accounting Principles and Reporting Practices*, London: Butterworths.

Puxty, A. G., Willmott, H. C., Cooper, D. J. and Lowe, A. (1987) 'Modes of regulation in advanced capitalism: locating accountancy in four countries', *Accounting, Organizations and Society*, 12 (3).

Ryan, J. B. (1985) 'Book review of *International Classification of Financial Reporting*', *Accounting and Finance*, November, pp. 87–8.

Saunders, M. R. (1977) *Tax Planning for Business in Europe*, London: Butterworths.

Seidler, L. J. (1967) 'International accounting – the ultimate theory course', *Accounting Review*, October.

Semler, J. (1962) 'The German accountant's approach to safe-guarding investors' creditors' interests', paper at the Eighth International Congress of Accountants, reprinted in *Australian Accountant*, September 1964.

Shils, E. (1966) *Political Development in the New States*, The Hague: Moulton.

Shoenthal, E. (1989) 'Classification of accounting systems using competencies as a discriminatory variable: A Great Britain–United States Study', *Journal of Business Finance and Accounting*, Autumn.

Shoenthal, E. (1991) 'Classification by competencies: A reply', *Journal of Business Finance and Accounting*.

Sibley, S. (1981) 'Equity ownership: the sprats and dolphins', *Accountant's Magazine*, September.

Stamp, E. (1980) *Corporate Reporting: Its Future Evolution*, Toronto: Canadian Institute of Chartered Accountants.

Stillwell, M. (1976) *European Financial Reporting – 3*, ICAEW, 49.

Touche Ross (1989) *Accounting for Europe*.

van Waardenburg, D. A. (1979) 'France: The Finance Law, 1979', *European Taxation*, No. 4.

Walker, R. G. (1978) *Consolidated Statements*, Arno Press.

Watts, R. L. and Zimmerman, J. L. (1979) 'The demand for and the supply of accounting theories; the market for excuses', *Accounting Review*, April, 301.

Zeff, S. A. (1972) *Forging Accounting Principles in Five Countries*, Champaign, Illinois: Stripes Publishers.

Zeff, S. A. (1979) *Forging Accounting Principles in New Zealand*, Wellington: Victoria University Press.

Index